COMPUTERS, INTERNET, AND SOCIETY

Privacy, Security, and Cyberspace

COMPUTERS, INTERNET, AND SOCIETY

Privacy, Security, and Cyberspace

Robert Plotkin

Facts On File
An Infobase Learning Company

PRIVACY, SECURITY, AND CYBERSPACE

Facts On File, Inc.
An imprint of Infobase Learning
132 West 31st Street
New York NY 10001

Library of Congress Cataloging-in-Publication Data

Plotkin, Robert, 1971–
    Privacy, security, and cyberspace / Robert Plotkin.
        p. cm.—(Computers, internet, and society)
    Includes bibliographical references and index.
    ISBN 978-0-8160-7756-4 (acid-free paper) 1. Computer security—Juvenile literature. 2. Computer viruses—Juvenile literature. 3. Spyware (Computer software)—Juvenile literature. 4. Social engineering—Juvenile literature. I. Title.
    QA76.9.A25P595 2012
    005.8—dc22   2011006927

Facts On File books are available at special discounts when purchased in bulk quantities for businesses, associations, institutions, or sales promotions. Please call our Special Sales Department in New York at (212) 967-8800 or (800) 322-8755.

You can find Facts On File on the World Wide Web at http://www.infobaselearning.com

Excerpts included herewith have been reprinted by permission of the copyright holders; the author has made every effort to contact copyright holders. The publishers will be glad to rectify, in future editions, any errors or omissions brought to their notice.

Text design by Kerry Casey
Composition by Hermitage Publishing Services
Illustrations by Bobbi McCutcheon
Photo research by Suzanne M. Tibor
Cover printed by Yurchak Printing, Landisville, Pa.
Book printed and bound by Yurchak Printing, Landisville, Pa.
Date printed: March 2012

Printed in the United States of America

This book is printed on acid-free paper.

3 4859 00344 6712

CONTENTS

PREFACE

Computers permeate innumerable aspects of people's lives. For example, computers are used to communicate with friends and family, analyze finances, play games, watch movies, listen to music, purchase products and services, and learn about the world. People increasingly use computers without even knowing it, as microprocessors containing software replace mechanical and electrical components in everything from automobiles to microwave ovens to wristwatches.

Conversations about computers tend to focus on their technological features, such as how many billions of calculations they can perform per second, how much memory they contain, or how small they have become. We have good reason to be amazed at advances in computer technology over the last 50 years. According to one common formulation of Moore's law (named after Gordon Moore of Intel Corporation), the number of transistors on a chip doubles roughly every two years. As a result, a computer that can be bought for $1,000 today is as powerful as a computer that cost more than $1 million just 15 years ago.

Although such technological wonders are impressive in their own right, we care about them not because of the engineering achievements they represent but because they have changed how people interact every day. E-mail not only enables communication with existing friends and family more quickly and less expensively but also lets us forge friendships with strangers halfway across the globe. Social networking platforms such as Twitter and Facebook enable nearly instant, effortless communication among large groups of people without requiring the time or effort needed to compose and read e-mail messages. These and other forms of communication are facilitated by increasingly powerful mobile handheld devices, such as the BlackBerry and iPhone, which make it possible for people to communicate at any time and in any place, thereby eliminating the need for a desktop computer with a hardwired Internet connection. Such improvements in technology have led to changes in society, often in complex and unexpected ways.

Understanding the full impact that computers have on society therefore requires an appreciation of not only what computers can do but also how computer technology is used in practice and its effects on human behavior and attitudes.

Computers, Internet, and Society is a timely multivolume set that seeks to provide students with such an understanding. The set includes the following six titles, each of which focuses on a particular context in which computers have a significant social impact:

- *Communication and Cyberspace*
- *Computer Ethics*
- *Computers and Creativity*
- *Computers in Science and Mathematics*
- *Computers in the Workplace*
- *Privacy, Security, and Cyberspace*

It is the goal of each volume to accomplish the following:

- explain the history of the relevant computer technology, what such technology can do today, and how it works;
- explain how computers interact with human behavior in a particular social context; and
- encourage readers to develop socially responsible attitudes and behaviors in their roles as computer users and future developers of computer technology.

New technology can be so engrossing that people often adopt it—and adapt their behavior to it—quickly and without much forethought. Yesterday's students gathered in the schoolyard to plan for a weekend party; today they meet online on a social networking Web site. People flock to such new features as soon as they come available, as evidenced by the long lines at the store every time a newer, smarter phone is announced.

Most such developments are positive. Yet they also carry implications for our privacy, freedom of speech, and security, all of which are easily overlooked if one does not pause to think about them. The paradox of today's computer technology is that it is both everywhere and invisible. The goal of this set is to make such technology visible so that it, and its impact on society, can be examined, as well as to assist students in using conceptual tools for making informed and responsible decisions about how to both apply and further develop that technology now and as adults.

Although today's students are more computer savvy than all of the generations that preceded them, many students are more familiar with what computers can do than with how computers work or the social changes being wrought by computers. Students who use the Internet constantly may remain unaware of how computers can be used to invade their privacy or steal their identity or how journalists and human rights activists use computer encryption technology to keep their communications secret and secure from oppressive governments around the world. Students who have grown up copying information from the World Wide Web and downloading songs, videos, and feature-length films onto computers, iPods, and cell phones may not understand the circumstances under which those activities are legitimate and when they violate copyright law. And students who have only learned about scientists and inventors in history books probably are unaware that today's innovators are using computers to discover new drugs and write pop music at the touch of a button.

In fact, young people have had such close and ongoing interactions with computers since they were born that they often lack the historical perspective to understand just how much computers have made their lives different from those of their parents. Computers form as much of the background of students' lives as the air they breathe; as a result, they tend to take both for granted. This set, therefore, is highly relevant and important to students because it enables them to understand not only how computers work but also how computer technology has affected their lives. The goal of this set is to provide students with the intellectual tools needed to think critically about computer technology so that they can make informed and responsible decisions about how to both use and further develop that technology now and as adults.

This set reflects my long-standing personal and professional interest in the intersection between computer technology, law, and society. I started programming computers when I was about 10 years old and my fascination with the technology has endured ever since. I had the honor of studying computer science and engineering at the Massachusetts Institute of Technology (MIT) and then studying law at the Boston University School of Law, where I now teach a course entitled, "Software and the Law." Although I spend most of my time as a practicing patent lawyer, focusing on patent protection for computer technology, I have also spoken and written internationally on topics including patent protection for software, freedom of speech, electronic privacy, and ethical implications of releasing potentially harmful software. My book, *The Genie in the Machine,* explores the impact of computer-automated inventing on law, businesses, inventors, and consumers.

What has been most interesting to me has been to study not any one aspect of computer technology, but rather to delve into the wide range of ways in which such technology affects, and is affected by, society. As a result, a multidisciplinary set such as this is a perfect fit for my background and interests. Although it can be challenging to educate non-technologists about how computers work, I have written and spoken about such topics to audiences including practicing lawyers, law professors, computer scientists and engineers, ethicists, philosophers, and historians. Even the work that I have targeted solely to lawyers has been multidisciplinary in nature, drawing on the history and philosophy of computer technology to provide context and inform my legal analysis. I specifically designed my course on "Software and the Law" to be understandable to law students with no background in computer technology. I have leveraged this experience in explaining complex technical concepts to lay audiences in the writing of this multidisciplinary set for a student audience in a manner that is understandable and engaging to students of any background.

The world of computers changes so rapidly that it can be difficult even for those of us who spend most of our waking hours learning about the latest developments in computer technology to stay up to date. The term *technological singularity* has even been coined to refer to a point, perhaps not too far in the future, when the rate of technological change will become so rapid that essentially no time elapses between one technological advance and the next. For better or worse, time does elapse between writing a series of books such as this and the date of publication. With full awareness of the need to provide students with current and relevant information, every effort has been made, up to the time at which these volumes are shipped to the printers, to ensure that each title in this set is as up to date as possible.

ACKNOWLEDGMENTS

Many people deserve thanks for making this series a reality. First, my thanks to my literary agent, Jodie Rhodes, for introducing me to Facts On File. When she first approached me, it was to ask whether I knew any authors who were interested in writing a series of books on a topic that I know nothing about—I believe it was biology. In response, I asked whether there might be interest in a topic closer to my heart—computers and society—and, as they say, the rest is history.

Frank Darmstadt, my editor, has not only held my hand through all of the high-level planning and low-level details involved in writing a series of this magnitude, but also he exhibited near superhuman patience in the face of drafts whose separation in time could be marked by the passing of the seasons. He also helped me to toe the fine dividing line between the forest and the trees and between today's technological marvels and tomorrow's long-forgotten fads—a distinction that is particularly difficult to draw in the face of rapidly changing technology.

Several research assistants, including Catie Watson, Rebekah Judson, Jessica McElrath, Sue Keeler, Samuel Smith, and Kristen Lighter, provided invaluable aid in uncovering and summarizing information about technologies ranging from the ancient to the latest gadgets we carry in our pockets. In particular, Luba Jabsky performed extensive research that formed the foundation of many of the book's chapters and biographies.

As the saying goes, a picture is worth a thousand words, and this set comes to life through the artwork and photographs it contains. Although computer science, with its microscopic electronic components and abstract software modules, is a particularly difficult field to illustrate visually, artist Bobbi McCutcheon and photo research Suzie Tibor could not have matched visuals to text more perfectly.

Last, but not least, I thank my family, including my partner, Melissa, and my dog, Maggie, for standing by my side and at my feet, respectively, as I spent my evenings and weekends trying, through words and pictures, to convey some of the wonder and excitement in computer technology that I felt as a teenager.

INTRODUCTION

Digital technology is causing governments, businesses, and individuals to rethink long-held notions of privacy and security. *Privacy, Security, and Cyberspace* is a book that both traces the history of privacy and security *and* explores the variety of ways in which computer and Internet technology can be used both to enhance privacy and security and to invade privacy and breach security.

For example, extensive government *databases* and the increased use of the Internet for text, audio, and video communication make it possible to monitor every Web site a computer user visits and every conversation that they have. Although such monitoring can be used to perform surveillance on actual or suspected criminals, it can also be used to spy on innocent individuals if sufficient technological and legal constraints are not in place. Many of the laws that govern privacy were written before the advent of computers or during the early years of the Internet and have since become outdated. Although individuals and organizations can use technology to keep their data private and secure, those who seek to access and steal such data are always developing new *computer viruses,* scams, and other techniques in an attempt to stay one step ahead of computer security experts. As a result, digital privacy and security often became a cat-and-mouse game in which owners of computers and digital data constantly update their defenses in response to new threats, while black hat hackers then develop new ways to break through such defenses.

Chapter 1 focuses on the legal *right to privacy* as interpreted by judges, legislators, and law enforcement. It addresses questions such as whether it is lawful for law enforcement to access logs of Internet data, e-mail messages, or the browsing history of individuals and at what point the fight against terrorism online becomes an invasion of personal privacy. Evolving technology presents an ever-changing demand for new legislation, and this chapter discusses some of the ways in which legislation for protecting electronic privacy currently falls short of the mark and is in the process of being updated for the digital age.

Chapter 2 discusses viruses and *malware.* A history of devastating viral outbreaks, including the early Internet *worms* Melissa and ILOVEYOU, illustrates the severity of these attacks, some causing upward of $10 billion in damages. The battle between the malfeasants who create these attacks and the security companies, like Symantec, who are tasked with defending against them has escalated into all-out war of evolving, nearly undetectable viruses and heuristic detection, often identifying a virus from no more than the few bits of code found in its every strain.

Chapter 3 introduces readers to *spyware,* a broad term used to describe software that is covertly installed on computers to gather information without the user's knowledge or permission. Spyware typically monitors how a computer is being used, including which Web sites are visited. It may even track keystrokes and mouse clicks, allowing a third party to collect user names and passwords and other personal information.

Chapter 4 introduces confidence schemes in the computer era. It demonstrates how scammers can cause widespread damage to a network without a virus or a worm. *Social engineers*—hackers who attempt to con users out of their passwords and other sensitive information—attack the most insecure layer of data security—the user in front of the computer. This chapter discusses common scams, from variants of the *Nigerian scam* to the exploits of Kevin Mitnick, who conned his way into systems ranging from Pacific Bell telecom mainframes to, allegedly, even FBI and Pentagon networks.

Chapter 5 discusses the benefits and costs of the huge repository of information that is the Internet. The chapter explains the risks to privacy and security of providing information online, especially on social networks, and how to make responsible decisions about what information should be kept private.

Chapter 6 discusses identity theft and the variety of methods used by thieves to gather the necessary documents for obtaining credit cards or even passports under a false name. Prominent examples of identity fraud, including the theft of 40 million credit cards from retailers such as Target and Office Max, illustrate the devastating consequences that can result from neglecting to shred important documents or using insecure passwords.

Chapter 7 examines ways to keep electronic data secure by using *encryption* technology, how to maintain the security of backup copies of data, and the particular challenges of keeping wireless networks secure. The chapter concludes by recommending ways to maintain privacy and security when using public computers and when using private computers to connect to public networks.

Chapter 8 is an in-depth examination of the implications of database technology for privacy. Although many databases containing information about people are created using information provided by those people themselves, other databases gather information from public records and other existing electronic sources. Although databases containing electronic medical records can be of immense benefit to both doctors and patients, such data must be kept highly secure to avoid exposing the most sensitive private medical information about patients. It is particularly challenging to maintain privacy in the face of an increasing number of interconnected databases. Even when personally identifying information is stripped from each individual database, it is sometimes possible to combine such databases and reidentify the individuals represented within the databases.

The World Wide Web is a vast repository of information accessible by anyone from anywhere in the world. It was designed to make information as easily available as possible. As a result, neither privacy nor security protections were designed into it from the outset. Furthermore, many technological advances on the Web and the Internet more generally are driven by the desire to make a wider variety of information available to more people more easily. Therefore, privacy and security often are not addressed when implementing new features or are added in as an afterthought. Furthermore, even when the best effort is made to protect the privacy and security of electronic data, oversights and limitations in existing technology can leave open gaps that can be exploited to invade privacy or breach security. Afterward it usually is not possible to recover the stolen idea and make it private once again. One take-home message from *Privacy, Security, and Cyberspace* is that sometimes sensitive information belongs on a computer that is not connected to the Internet at all, because once the information is published online, it is on the public record forever.

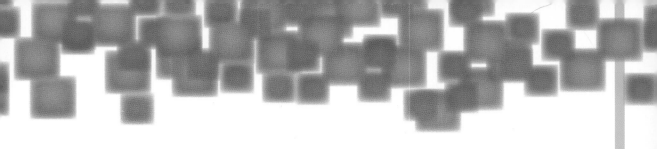

1

YOUR RIGHT TO PRIVACY

In the United States, the Constitution is a guaranteed protector of certain unalienable rights, including the right to freedom of speech, the right to freedom of religion, protections from unlawful searches and seizures, the right to due process, and others, all of which are specifically granted by the first 10 amendments to the Constitution, known as the Bill of Rights. Nowhere, however, does the Constitution specifically mention a right to privacy. Instead, the set of rights that has come to be known as the right to privacy has evolved over the years as Congress has passed new laws, the Supreme Court has settled court cases, and law enforcement has tested the boundaries of personal privacy in its pursuit of criminals. It is precisely because the Constitution does not expressly grant a right to privacy that the exact contours of this right—and even its existence—remain controversial.

This chapter will address the history of the right to privacy in the United States. It will discuss the foundations of the right to privacy, including the court cases and statutes that have granted privacy rights. Finally, this chapter explains how these rights need to adapt in order to protect the privacy of electronic data.

ORIGINS OF THE FOURTH AMENDMENT

The Fourth Amendment to the Constitution guarantees people's "right to be secure in their persons, houses, papers, and effects, against unreasonable searches and seizures." Although this right was not conferred to the colonists before the American Revolution, this idea of personal freedom dates back to England, where a man was master of his house and could defend his home from unlawful entry by anyone, even a king's agent. This freedom was

1

set aside in the colonies, where British soldiers attempted to rein in smuggling and avoidance of taxes through the use of *general warrants* and *writs of assistance* to enter and search any house. General warrants gave authorization for a broad search for evidence of any crime and did not mention items to be seized or places within a home to be searched. A writ of assistance was a general warrant, which, once issued, remained valid as long as the sovereign who signed it was alive and for an additional six months following his death. When King George II

Invasion of private homes by British soldiers before the founding of the United States was one of the primary grievances of the colonists against the British government, leading to a prohibition in the U.S. Constitution of the quartering (housing) of British troops in the homes of American colonists. This illustration shows British soldiers plundering an American colonial home in the years leading up to the American Revolution. *(North Wind Picture Archives/Alamy)*

died in 1760 and British authorities were required to obtain new writs, colonists, led by James Otis, attacked the issuance on grounds of the writs' invalidity and incompatibility with English laws. They lost, and the writs were reissued, but this experience prompted the drafters of the Constitution to include an amendment that guaranteed individual freedom from such practices.

The Founding Fathers viewed general warrants as a violation of an individual's natural right to protect himself and his home. The Bill of Rights was drafted and adopted out of a desire to provide more clear and express protection for individual rights. Although no constitutional amendment specifically mentions a right to privacy, the right provided by the Fourth Amendment to protection from unlawful searches and seizures is a protection against invasion of one's private space by the government. The Third Amendment protects the privacy of the household. The Fifth Amendment provides privacy for those threatened with self-incrimination. Based on these amendments, it seems undeniable that the framers of the Constitution intended to protect individual privacy.

The U.S. Supreme Court has interpreted these rights in different ways in different times. One of the first large expansions to the right of privacy came in 1965 in the landmark case of *Griswold v. Connecticut* (381 U.S. 479). In *Griswold,* the Court decided the right to privacy was protected under a "penumbra of rights," that is, it was clear from the Founding Fathers' intentions that there should be a right to privacy, even if such a right was not expressly stated in the Constitution. In the years since *Griswold,* the Supreme Court has decided many additional cases in which it has recognized more clearly the right to privacy granted by the Fourth Amendment and the Constitution. Through these cases, the Supreme Court has protected a right to personal security and liberty and, most important, the right to be left alone.

EVOLUTION OF PRIVACY PROTECTIONS FOR NEW TECHNOLOGIES

Although the Fourth Amendment originally protected physical privacy, such as freedom from unlawful entry and search and seizure of property, with the advent of new technologies the concept of what privacy is and is not has expanded. The right to privacy in the modern, technologically advanced world is more than a guarantee of protection from governmental intrusion. Instead, the right to privacy has evolved to include the right of a person to control the personal information that is disclosed to the government or is made available to corporations and other private entities.

Telegraph

In the 19th century, the telegraph became a popular means of communication. (See *Communication and Cyberspace* in this set.) The invention of the telegraph gave rise to the first questions of data privacy. No longer were messages passed privately from one person to another. Instead, because telegraph operators were required to serve as intermediaries to transmit and receive every telegraph message, such operators became privy to information that was meant to be kept private.

Although everyone agreed that telegraph operators were supposed to keep telegraph messages confidential, telegraph operators often revealed messages about criminal activities to the police. Telegraph operators were often *subpoenaed* in lawsuits and required to reveal the contents of the messages they handled in court. Anyone who had sent a telegraph about crimes could be prosecuted. Even when telegraph operators attempted to uphold their civil duty to keep telegraph messages private, the government did not recognize the privacy of such messages. As a result, telegraph messages remained relatively difficult to keep private throughout the 19th century. Letters, which required a warrant to intercept, were far more secure.

Telephone

In the early years of the telephone, switchboard operators still connected calls, but they disconnected from the line after the caller was connected. As a result, even if law enforcement were to subpoena a switchboard operator to testify in court, the operator would have no information about the content of the call. Technology for listening to telephone calls, however, continued to advance. Eventually, police learned that they could tap into telephone conversations and listen to or record them using wiretapping equipment. A *pen register* is a device that, once attached to a telephone, could record all of the phone numbers dialed from that telephone. The FBI used pen registers to conduct surveillance in the early days of the telephone. As a result, many people were arrested and convicted based on the content of their telephone conversations and the identities of the

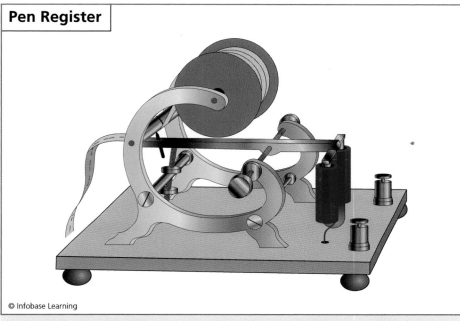

Pen Register

© Infobase Learning

A pen register is a device that records all telephone numbers dialed from a particular telephone line. This is in contrast to a trap-and-trace device, which records all telephone numbers of incoming calls received by a particular telephone line. Pen registers and trap-and-trace devices are used commonly in criminal surveillance.

people they spoke with. In the landmark 1967 case *Katz v. United States* (389 U.S. 347), the right of privacy expanded to prevent eavesdropping in the form of wiretaps by law enforcement officials.

Charles Katz was arrested after he used a payphone in California to place illegal bets in Massachusetts and Florida. He was convicted based on the FBI's recording of his conversation using a recording device placed on the exterior of the phone booth. Katz appealed, arguing that the recording violated his Fourth Amendment right against unreasonable search and seizure. In response, the FBI maintained that recording was permissible because no physical intrusion into Katz's home took place and that, therefore, the protections of the Fourth Amendment did not apply. According to Justice Stewart, evidence obtained by the police falls within the protection of the Fourth Amendment if: (1) a person expected that the information was to be kept private; and (2) society is prepared to recognize such expectation as reasonable. Katz believed his conversation in the telephone booth would be private, as would any reasonable member of society. The Court held that the Fourth Amendment protects people, not places. For this reason, Katz's private telephone conversation could not be used to convict him of illegal gambling. The Supreme Court reversed the lower court's decision and decided in favor of Katz, concluding that the FBI's wiretapping constituted a "search" under the Fourth Amendment and violated Katz's right to privacy.

Databases

The technology of information scanning and retrieval has improved. Whereas law enforcement used to keep information in paper files, requiring clerks to search through stored records by hand, now they have access to national fingerprint, DNA, driver's license, and criminal history databases, searchable in minutes. Other industries use national databases as well. Supermarkets and retailers compile data on what customers purchase by offering incentives like discounts or coupons for shoppers with store cards.

It is obvious that these databases are important, and the technology is more beneficial than harmful. Unfortunately, they also provide a perfect opportunity for identity theft by unscrupulous employees or hackers. Like some technological innovations, the law has been slow to provide protection against those who abuse database technology. A few states, such as Massachusetts, have passed laws requiring database owners to disclose information about their databases, including breaches in security, to users who are at risk of having their identities compromised. Other laws, like the Health Insurance Portability and Accountability Act (HIPAA) of 1996, which regulates the disclosure of health care or medical records, show that Congress recognizes the privacy of medical databases. Outside of these instances, there is little or no regulation of data privacy in databases.

Europeans are familiar with the damage that can be caused by unregulated personal information from their experiences during World War II, when fascist governments routinely used national databases in their efforts to evict, arrest, or seize property based on a disclosure of ethnicity or race. In the years following World War II, Europe supported comprehensive data protection laws. The Data Protection Directive regulates personal data within the European Union, requiring transparency in the collection, processing, and use of identifying information.

With the advent of the Internet, privacy laws must be expanded to include stored data about a person, including demographic information, browsing habits, and purchasing behavior. Europe has already enacted a number of laws that allow a person to control the data that companies have access to, limiting it or eliminating it if that is his or her desire. Though the government and corporations have built large databases about individuals in the population, Congress has not yet passed data privacy laws to protect and control these databases.

Internet

In 1986, foreseeing the upcoming personal computer revolution, Congress passed the Electronic Communications Privacy Act (ECPA). The goal of the ECPA was to extend the restrictions on law enforcement from *Katz v. United States* to include limitations on the ways in which law enforcement could access electronic data stored and transmitted by computers. Unfortunately, keeping any law up-to-date in a dynamic and ever-changing environment such as the Internet is extremely difficult for a Congress that was designed to pass laws slowly and where such laws are intended to remain in place unchanged for many years.

In fact, the ECPA is already outdated. For instance, the ECPA makes it illegal to intercept e-mail while it is in transmission but not to access stored e-mail. In 1986, when the ECPA was drafted, e-mails and access logs were not stored in the same way as they are now. E-mails were deleted from servers as they were downloaded. Logs were routinely removed after days or weeks. It was safe to assume, in 1986, that an e-mail account containing e-mails more than six months old had been abandoned. For this reason, the ECPA includes a provision according to which e-mails older than six months old may be accessed and read by law enforcement without a warrant. Now, however, most people store their e-mails forever, whether on their home computers or online in *cloud-based services* such as Gmail and Hotmail. The ECPA allows law enforcement to access e-mails stored in such accounts without a warrant because the drafters of the ECPA did not predict that e-mail technology would change in this way.

Proponents of Internet freedom and electronic privacy fear that law enforcement will abuse these provisions. They recommend that lawmakers modernize the ECPA with provisions such as requiring a warrant to conduct data surveillance, preventing unsupervised electronic snooping in the same way that the Fourth Amendment outlawed general warrants. When changes in technology outpace the law, any laws enacted will eventually become confusing and difficult to interpret, creating uncertainty for all involved.

LEGAL PROTECTION OF ELECTRONIC PRIVACY TODAY

In recent years, privacy protections were significantly weakened by the USA PATRIOT (United and Strengthening America by Providing Appropriate Tools Required to Intercept and Obstruct Terrorism) Act, which was passed by the U.S. Congress in 2001 in response to the terrorist attacks on September 11, 2001. To combat terrorism, lawmakers saw a need to allow some surveillance of electronic data without meeting the stringent requirements of the wiretap laws. Specifically, the PATRIOT Act allows surveillance of packet-switched networks and stored voice mail with a search warrant. Unlike in a traditional criminal investigation, probable cause is not required to obtain a search warrant for those suspected of terrorism. If subpoenaed, the PATRIOT Act requires cable companies to provide the FBI with information about users' Web browsing habits, including stored information and access logs. In response to a subpoena, Internet service providers (ISPs) are required to include users' names, addresses, telephone numbers, telephone records, length of service of a subscriber, session times and durations, client IP addresses, types of services used, and payment method, including bank account and credit card numbers. Libraries subpoenaed by the FBI are required to disclose library patron reading records and Web browsing history. Any right to privacy makes it more difficult for law enforcement to find and prosecute individuals suspected of a crime. In the case of terrorism, lawmakers made the decision to give up some rights for the security of the nation, whether or not this is what Benjamin Franklin had in mind when he wrote in 1759 in *An Historical Review of the Constitution and Government of Pennsylvania, From Its Origin,* "They that can give up essential liberty to obtain a little temporary safety deserve neither liberty nor safety."

THE EXPECTATION OF PRIVACY

In *Katz v. United States,* Justice Harlan described a two-part test for determining whether a government search is subject to the limitations of the Fourth Amendment. First, the individual must believe that the information seized was to be kept private, and, second, that expectation must be reasonable; that is, society must agree with him.

It is this second requirement that is most often called into question in court. In general, one cannot have a reasonable expectation of privacy when one is in a public place or when one knows that other people are listening. For instance, it has been ruled that one's garbage, placed outside, is not protected by the Fourth Amendment. The police are also allowed to trace the telephone numbers that are dialed from a telephone without a search warrant, although they need a warrant to listen to the resulting telephone conversations themselves.

Currently, courts are forging new ground in expectation of privacy cases regarding computers. In 2005, a court found that explicitly named computer files are probable cause for searching the computer. Employees using a workplace computer at a private company have little to no guarantee of privacy. Many employers create a legally binding statement of policy regarding monitoring of the workplace computers. If an employee signs the statement, he consents to whatever the statement says. Additionally, if e-mail service is provided to employees by the company and not by some third-party service such as Gmail or America Online, employees cannot expect their e-mails to be kept private. As a result, employers have the legal right to read the e-mails of their employees, even without notifying employees that they are doing so. On the other hand, employers who routinely or offensively overstep reasonable bounds, such as by publishing of personal e-mails of employees, may be successfully sued by employees in every state.

The fact is that e-mail is never truly private. People can forward it without one's permission. Law enforcement can look at it without a warrant after six months. Hackers can break into it. According to the technology lawyer Mark A. Bermin, "E-mails should more properly be viewed as a postcard or a conversation over a speakerphone, both open and available to a passerby to hear or see, than like a private letter."

If workplace e-mail is not protected by an expectation of privacy, then it would be reasonable that e-mail and laptops provided by a school could similarly be monitored by a school administration. This was the logic behind issuing laptops to students at a Pennsylvania public high school that were programmed to snap pictures randomly from the laptop's webcam. The school district believed that, since the laptops were school property, monitoring their whereabouts in case of theft or illegal activity was the school's right. Privacy advocates believed

(continues on page 12)

00110101010010101001110101101010101011001010100001

Justice Louis Brandeis, Supreme Court Justice

Born on November 13, 1856, in Lou-
isville, Kentucky, to Jewish immigrant
parents from Prague, Louis Dembitz
Brandeis went on to become a distin-
guished legal scholar, public advocate,
and Supreme Court justice. Although
he enrolled in Harvard Law School
without a formal college degree,
Brandeis graduated in 1877, a few
months before his 21st birthday, as
the youngest-ever class valedictorian,
causing Harvard to overlook its graduation requirement that one be at least
21 years old to obtain a law degree.
After graduation, Brandeis entered into
private practice in St. Louis and Boston and taught courses at Harvard Law
School and the Massachusetts Institute
of Technology.

Justice Louis Brandeis was responsible
for advancing the concept of a right
to privacy. *(Library of Congress)*

Early in his career, Brandeis
became involved in advancing the
causes of the socially and economically disadvantaged, earning the name of "the
People's Attorney." He undertook the majority of this work free of charge or at his
own expense, often billing himself to compensate his firm for the time he spent
working on these cases. However, it was not just the altruistic element of his work
that was remarkable but the way in which these cases affected and developed the
legal field. Brandeis's brief in *Muller v. Oregon* (1908) argued that minimum-hours
laws for women were constitutional, relying on sociological, statistical, scientific,
and economic data outlined in his brief. This "Brandeis brief," as it became known,
revolutionized the practice of brief-writing by presenting an overwhelming level
of factual detail to illustrate legal concepts. The brief consisted of more than 100
pages of statistical evidence supporting the final conclusion. It became a model for

00110101010010101001110101101010101011001010100001

legal defenses of and attack against public policy, in the way that it demonstrated the importance of laying a factual foundation for policy recommendations.

Another seminal work, an article entitled "The Right to Privacy," written together with Brandeis's frequent collaborator and partner Samuel Warren, was published in the *Harvard Law Review* in 1890. In this article, and later in his dissent in *Olmstead v. U.S.* (1928), Brandeis argued that the most valued human right is the "right to be left alone," a right to privacy and self-determination. This essay examined the development of various rights and liberties, from the most basic, such as physical safety, to less tangible but related rights, such as intellectual property and trademarks. The article concluded that the concept of privacy had changed over time. While privacy may have originated as a freedom from physical intrusion or harm, as technological progress allowed for lives more full of intellectual activity, the products of the intellect and the workings of the intellect had become just as sacred as the physical being. The law merely adjusted to protect these intellectual capacities for the same reasons that it initially protected more basic freedoms. This essay laid a foundation for subsequent Supreme Court cases recognizing a legal right to privacy, including *Roe v. Wade* and *Lawrence v. Texas*.

A passionate educator, Brandeis continued to include extensive factual descriptions in his famous dissents as a Supreme Court justice, using them as tools to educate not only his colleagues but also the American public. Brandeis's dissents, disliked by many of his fellow attorneys for their wordiness, provided a road map for legal reformers with their extensive use of facts to illustrate how a piece of legislation may be interpreted. Brandeis took delight in making his opinions instructive as well as persuasive and using his position to educate the public as well as members of the legal profession. He gave preference to selecting law clerks who demonstrated interest in becoming teachers, and about half of them did, carrying Brandeis's philosophy to future generations.

Although he had previously showed little interest in Jewish affairs, Brandeis became involved in the Zionist movement during World War I. An advocate of social and economic reforms and an opponent of industrial and financial monopoly, Brandeis contributed to the crafting of the economic doctrine of the New Freedom that was adopted by President Woodrow Wilson in his campaign in 1912. Brandeis was Wilson's choice for the position of Secretary of Commerce, but due

(continues)

001101010010100111010110101010101011001010000 1

(continued)

to intense political opposition, a tamer candidate was chosen. Brandeis remained an unofficial adviser to Wilson and was appointed to the Supreme Court in 1916, becoming the first Jewish justice in the history of the Court. His appointment was met with opposition from many anti-Semitic and business interests, who were alienated by Brandeis's liberal leanings and work for social reform. Justice Brandeis often dissented from the majority of the Court together with another liberal Justice, Oliver Wendell Holmes, Jr. Brandeis retired from the bench in 1939 and died in Washington, D.C., in 1941. Brandeis University in Waltham, Massachusetts, is named after him.

001101010010100111010110101010101011001010000 1

(continued from page 9)

that taking pictures of students without their consent, sometimes in their bedrooms, was a violation of privacy. When a student suspected of taking drugs was expelled after the pictures were seen by an administrator, the student sued the school. Whether or not this was an invasion of privacy was never addressed, because the school district settled with the plaintiff before the case went to court.

It is clear that the expectation of privacy varies over time and from situation to situation. The legal protection of privacy will continue to evolve in response to changes in technology. In some cases, the answers are clear. E-mail that is older than six months old should not be a matter of public record. In other cases, the questions are harder to answer. The law still has not decided whether a school district should be able to protect its property, such as a laptop, by monitoring pictures and videos taken using the laptop's webcam.

CONCLUSIONS

Individuals' concept of privacy is not always the same as the privacy that is protected by law. One reason is that laws tend to be written against a backdrop of particular technologies and to embody assumptions about how these technologies can affect privacy. When technology changes while the law does not, a disconnect can arise between how people view their own privacy and the extent to which the law protects such privacy. Even though the U.S. Constitution is intended to be a living document that is flexible enough to adapt to evolving circumstances, it is only reinterpreted in response to specific lawsuits that come before the courts. Many years may pass between lawsuits. As a result, there can be a significant time lag between the adoption of new technology and corresponding changes in how the Constitution is applied to the effects of such technology on privacy. Sometimes, this means that there is a period of time during which the government, private parties, or both can use technology to invade the privacy of others without violating the law. Other times, the gap between the law and reality imposes unnecessary restrictions on how new technologies can be used to engage in legitimate law enforcement activities.

One solution to this problem is for the Congress or the legislatures in individual states to pass new statutes to reflect new technological realities. Legislatures can act more quickly than courts and can address a wide range of situations, instead of being limited to handling only specific disputes between particular parties. As a result, legislatures have the potential to ensure that the law of privacy does not become outdated. At the same time, legislatures cannot predict the future. They are limited to acting based on their understanding of technology as it exists at the time they write new laws. As a result, any new laws run the risk of becoming obsolete soon after they are written. Although legislatures can attempt to forestall this outcome by writing laws that are very general in nature, such as laws that prohibit government agencies from unreasonably invading the privacy of individuals, such laws merely beg the question of what constitutes an unreasonable invasion of privacy in contrast to a reasonable one. Any dispute over what such terms mean must be resolved by the courts. Therefore, writing laws using general terms in an attempt to avoid technological obsolescence increases the likelihood that the laws will be challenged in court and potentially invalidated as a result of being held unconstitutional.

Given these difficulties, both judges and lawmakers do the best that they can to adjust the law of privacy to fit the current state of technology. Even with their best efforts, as long as computer and Internet technology continue to develop as quickly as they have over the last century, privacy law will continue to play catch-up so that it can maintain a balance between respecting the privacy of individuals and allowing governments and private entities to obtain personal information necessary to fulfill their missions.

2

COMPUTER VIRUSES: INVISIBLE THREATS TO PRIVACY

A computer virus is a software program that is designed to attack individual computers or computer networks. It is called a virus because it has the ability to automatically replicate itself and spread from one computer to another in the same way that a biological virus moves between organisms. Once a computer is infected by a virus, it will often be responsible for infecting other computers. Unlike biological viruses, computer viruses are created by humans for malicious purposes ranging from corrupting or stealing data to disrupting computer networks. Viruses are one example of a category of software called malware, reflecting the fact that they are software written with malicious intent.

One important thing to remember about viruses is that they cannot physically damage a computer's hardware. Viruses are software-based and the damage they do is to the software of infected computers. Like biological viruses, computer viruses can vary in severity from relatively harmless to massively destructive. The most serious malware attacks may require a computer owner to spend large amounts of time and effort eradicating the virus or may require the services of a computer repair specialist. Even a virus that does not harm an individual computer can tie up a network as it replicates itself, affecting e-mail systems, banking services, and other critical operations.

In order to function as designed, a computer virus must be able to execute its program code. To facilitate virus execution, a programmer may embed a virus in a legitimate program, infecting a computer when the program is executed. A virus then uses various techniques to search for other programs to infect, whether on an individual computer or across a network.

TYPES OF COMPUTER VIRUSES

Computer viruses, like their biological counterparts, come in many varieties. Some of the most common forms of computer viruses are the following:

> *Program Virus.* These viruses infect executable files (such as those with .EXE or .SYS extensions). When a computer user unknowingly executes the infected program, the virus is activated and will begin to replicate itself. A common form of a program virus is an ActiveX virus, which can be activated when viewing a Web site in a Microsoft Web browser. Most program viruses are inserted into the program after the program is first distributed by the program's creator. For example, a virus author may download an uninfected program from a Web site, insert the virus into the program, and then upload the infected version of the program to another Web site. When users download what appears to be the original program from the second Web site, they instead unknowingly download the infected version.
>
> *Boot Sector Virus.* This type of virus changes what is known as the *boot sector* of a computer's hard drive, blocking access to data on the drive. A boot sector virus that disables operating system startup functions can make it impossible to use a computer at all.
>
> *Macro Virus.* A virus can be spread through word processing or spreadsheet software by infecting documents that make use of the software's *macro* capability. A macro is a small piece of programming code that can be embedded into a document. For example, a macro in a word processing document might search through the document and indent the first line of every paragraph. *Macro viruses* make use of the ability of macros to execute program code automatically to perform harmful functions. When a document infected with a macro virus is opened, the virus embedded in the macro is executed automatically and often without any indication that it is running.
>
> *Bombs.* A logic *bomb* or time bomb virus is designed to execute on a specific date or when a specific event or action occurs. For example, a

disgruntled employee might create a bomb that is designed to delete important company files when the employee is fired or on the day before the company's tax returns are due to be filed.

Computer viruses are spread in a number of ways. They may be included in an e-mail attachment or instant message or transferred through *peer-to-peer (P2P)* file sharing or through Web site downloads. The portion of a virus program that is intended to harm an infected computer is often referred to as the *payload.* In most cases, an action on the part of a computer user is required to activate the payload and spread the virus, such as opening an e-mail attachment or executing a downloaded program.

Other types of malware are sometimes categorized as computer viruses. A computer worm is a malicious program that can replicate without human interaction by sending copies of itself to computers on a network. It is technically not a virus because it does not require any action by the computer user and does not attach itself to any existing program. Another type of malware is a *Trojan horse,* which is a software program that appears to perform a useful function but is actually malicious. The name is derived from the Trojan horse of Greek mythology, which was a large wooden horse that was presented to the Trojans by the Greeks. Although the horse appeared to be a gift, it hid 30 soldiers who exited the horse under cover of darkness and opened the city gates to the Greek army, who entered and destroyed the city. A recent example of a Trojan horse is a program that claimed to track the number of people who visit a Facebook user's home page. After asking for personal information, the program targeted the user with advertising rather than tracking visitors.

(opposite page) Computer viruses often spread using links in e-mail messages. This illustration shows an example in which an e-mail message contains a link to a virus. A user downloads the e-mail message over the Internet from an e-mail server to the user's computer, where the user opens the e-mail message and clicks on the link, thinking that the link points to a legitimate Web site. Instead, clicking on the link causes the user's computer to download a virus, which secretly installs itself on the user's computer and sends an identical e-mail to others over the Internet, without the user's knowledge. The process of infection repeats itself as additional users click on the link and thereby cause the virus to be installed on their computers and to be spread to yet other computers. Once installed on a computer, the virus may take other harmful action, such as deleting files or transmitting private information to the author of the virus.

(IN)FAMOUS COMPUTER VIRUSES

The first personal computer virus found "in the wild" (which means that it was put into general circulation) was a boot sector virus nicknamed (c)Brain. It originated in Pakistan in 1986 and was written by brothers Basit and Amjad

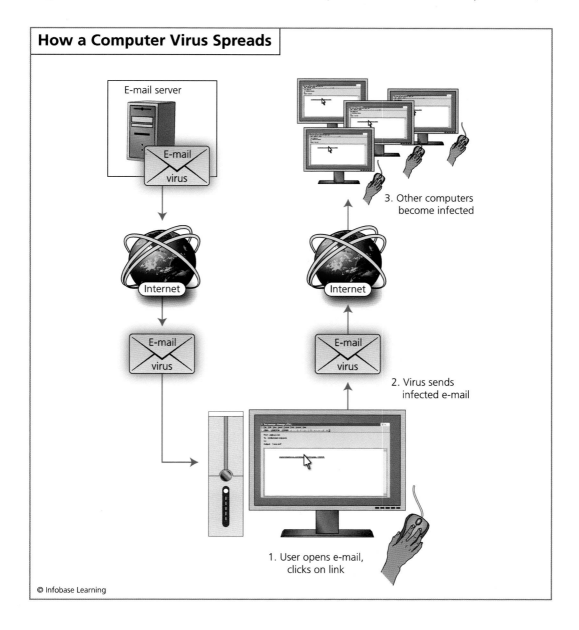

How a Computer Virus Spreads

E-mail server

E-mail virus

Internet

E-mail virus

1. User opens e-mail, clicks on link

2. Virus sends infected e-mail

3. Other computers become infected

Internet

E-mail virus

© Infobase Learning

Farooq Alvi, who owned a computer store named Brain Computer Service. They discovered that they could alter the boot sector of a floppy disk (the precursor to today's hard drive) that contained one of their software products. It is believed that they attempted to protect their software from *piracy* (illegal copying) by adding the name, address, and phone number of their store and a message telling users of the disk that their computer was infected with a virus. The (c)Brain virus did not appear to be malicious, but the Farooq Alvi brothers were soon flooded with phones calls from around the world requesting the antidote to their virus.

More malicious viruses soon followed (c)Brain. In the mid-1990s, as more computer users began to share word processing documents and spreadsheets, macro viruses began to appear. The Melissa virus, which was released in March 1999, has the distinction of being the first e-mail virus to have a global impact. The virus was embedded in a macro in a Microsoft Word document that was sent as an e-mail attachment. When a computer user received the Melissa e-mail, it appeared to have been sent by a friend or acquaintance. The e-mail message invited the recipient to check out the contents of the attached document. When the document was opened, the virus caused copies of the e-mail to be sent to the first 50 addresses in the recipient's e-mail contact list.

The Melissa virus was contained within a few days, but not before it had infected hundreds of thousands of computers, shut down the e-mail systems of many government agencies and large corporations, and caused an estimated $80 million in damages. David L. Smith, a New Jersey programmer who was the author of the Melissa virus, was arrested by the FBI within one week and eventually sentenced to a 20-month jail term.

On May 4, 2000, a little more than a year after the Melissa outbreak, a new major virus was unleashed. The ILOVEYOU virus (also known as LoveLetter and LoveBug) was named for the "I love you" subject line on the e-mail that spread it. This virus far surpassed Melissa in its circulation and impact. Like the Melissa virus, ILOVEYOU used an e-mail message to entice computer users to open an attachment. In this case, the attachment used Visual Basic Scripting (VBS) to deliver its payload. The ILOVEYOU virus was more aggressive and malicious than Melissa. In addition to using an infected computer's e-mail to resend itself to other computers, it overwrote system files and sent passwords and other secure information from infected computers to the author of the virus. In a little more than a week, more than 50 million infected computers had been reported. In addition to shutting down corporate e-mail, ILOVEYOU affected e-mail systems in the Pentagon, CIA, and British Parliament. Before it was stopped, the virus is estimated to have caused between $5 billion and $10 billion in damages.

The ILOVEYOU virus originated in the Philippines. It was tracked to a suspected author, a former university student named Onel de Guzman. Both de Guzman and a suspected coconspirator named Reomel Ramones were arrested but soon released due to the lack of laws in the Philippines against writing and distributing malware.

The first decade of the new millennium was marked by a series of massive computer virus and worm attacks. In the summer of 2001, a computer worm named Code Red exploited a Microsoft Windows vulnerability known as buffer overflow and attempted to launch an attack on the White House Web site. A time bomb in the virus instructed infected computers to access the Web site on a predetermined date and time. The virus author hoped that the volume of traffic would crash the site. Virus hunters discovered the bomb and notified the White House, which blocked Web site access. Code Red II, a second version of the virus, created a so-called backdoor into a computer's operating system that allowed an outsider to control the computer. By the time Microsoft released software patches to protect computers running Windows against Code Red worms, the malware had caused an estimated $2 billion in damages.

In September 2001, exactly one week after terrorist attacks on the World Trade Center and the Pentagon, a computer worm named Nimda was released. The name Nimda was derived from a reverse spelling of the common computer term *admin*. Because this worm had multiple attack methods and targeted computers and servers running any version of Windows, it spread very rapidly. Within 22 minutes of being released into the wild, it had become the most widespread virus or worm on the Internet. Its attack methods included e-mail, browsing compromised Web sites, exploiting Windows vulnerabilities, and even backdoors left by the Code Red II virus. Nimda's purpose was to propagate itself as quickly and as widely as possible, tying up networks and blocking Web sites. Its original author remains unknown, but in the months following its original release it was rereleased several times in slightly modified forms. The damages from Nimda are estimated to be about $500 million.

In January 2003, another fast-moving computer worm named Slammer (or SQL Slammer) attacked computers throughout the world. Slammer infected about 75,000 users in 10 minutes and caused a dramatic slowdown in Internet traffic. Like the Code Red worm, Slammer took advantage of a buffer overflow condition, this time in Microsoft's SQL Server. Then in January 2004, the MyDoom worm gained the title of fastest-spreading e-mail worm in history. MyDoom's suspected purpose was to send *spam advertising*. It was activated by opening an

The Melissa Virus

The Melissa virus was the first mass-mailing e-mail virus to have a worldwide impact. It was created by a 30-year-old network programmer living in New Jersey named David L. Smith. In the 1990s, criminals had not yet discovered that computer viruses and malware could be used for computer crime. Instead, isolated programmers created viruses to create havoc and gain fame. Melissa, which Smith named after an exotic dancer, had no malicious purpose other than to replicate itself through e-mail. However, the speed with which it replicated had a devastating effect on e-mail servers. The Melissa virus earned a place in computer virus history on March 26, 1999, when it flooded corporate network systems, infected hundreds of thousands of computers, and caused Microsoft, Intel, and other companies to temporarily shut down e-mail.

Melissa is categorized as a macro virus because the virus program code is embedded in a macro that is included in a Microsoft Word document. The document is attached to an e-mail message with the following subject header:

Subject: Important Message From <name>

Where <name> would be the name of someone usually known to the e-mail recipient. The message body of the e-mail consists of the following text:

Here is the document you asked for . . . don't show it to anyone else ;-)

If the e-mail recipient opens the attachment in Microsoft Word 97 or Word 2000, the virus is activated and attempts to replicate itself by forwarding the e-mail attachment, much like the ILOVEYOU virus. It then resent itself to e-mail contacts found on the infected computer and embedded itself in files that might be shared on peer-to-peer file-sharing systems. MyDoom attempted to launch several attacks on the Microsoft and Google Web sites and on other major Web sites, but its impact was minimized by detection and preventative measures.

In addition to the major viruses and worms described here, there were dozens of other attacks between 2000 and 2010. In November 2008, a new worm

e-mail to the first 50 addresses found in the computer's Outlook e-mail contact list. The computer user's name is used for <name> in the e-mail subject line, causing unsuspecting recipients to think the e-mail is from a trusted source. The virus infects the Normal.dot template used by Word, so that all of a user's documents that reference this template will become infected and will cause the virus to propagate when opened.

Because several large corporations were affected, the U.S. Department of Defense's Computer Emergency Response Team (CERT) was alerted. Through the timely efforts of McAfee Avert Labs and other computer security experts, detection and removal tools were quickly developed and the virus was for the most part contained within a few days. However, Melissa continued to infect individual computers for a long period after its containment. The overall damages from the Melissa virus were estimated to be $80 million.

David L. Smith launched the virus from a pirated AOL account. The FBI obtained information from AOL that identified Smith's computer and his apartment's telephone line as the source of the virus. He was arrested on April 2, 1999, and charged with interrupting public communication. Following a lengthy trial process, in 2002 he was fined $5,000 and sentenced to a 20-month jail term. In the months leading up to his trial, Smith cooperated with the FBI and identified other virus authors in order to reduce what could have been a prison sentence of 10 years and a $150,000 fine.

In reaction to Melissa and other macro viruses, newer versions of Microsoft Word, Excel, and Outlook were made less vulnerable to attack. Warning messages were added to alert users when they are about to open a document that contains macros. Users are also given the option of disabling macro execution until the document has been checked with *antivirus software*.

named Conficker surfaced. It targeted all versions of Microsoft server systems, from Windows 2000 to Windows 7. Its purpose was to take control of individual computers and allow them to be commanded remotely by the authors of the worm. Conficker uses a combination of malware techniques, making it difficult to eradicate. It has continued to spread to government, business, and home computers since it was launched and is now believed to control more than 7 million computers in more than 200 countries. In February 2009, Microsoft offered a $250,000 reward for the capture, arrest, and conviction of the individuals responsible for the creation and distribution of Conficker. The ultimate effect of Conficker remains unknown, but is suspected to be a worldwide infrastructure for cybercrime that may include identity theft, online scams, and spam.

WHY DO PEOPLE SPREAD VIRUSES?

A computer virus attack often feels like a personal attack. It can destroy important data and render a computer unusable. Private information can be stolen by a virus, leading to identity thefts and fraud. What kind of people devise and spread the computer viruses that cause so much damage?

In the early days of personal computers, writing and spreading a virus were seen as a challenge by some unethical programmers. These "digital vandals" were usually male teenagers or young adults. They were often part of an online forum or newsgroup where information about viruses was exchanged. An amateur programmer might create a new virus to impress his peers or gain some other form of recognition. Since digital vandals were often self-taught programmers, the viruses they produced were often unpredictable. They might fail to cause the intended damage, or they might be far more destructive than planned.

Following the attention given to major viruses like Melissa and ILOVEYOU, a new class of virus writers emerged. A greater number of professional programmers began to write virus software, using their expertise to take advantage of vulnerabilities in Microsoft Windows and other computer operating systems and applications. Today's virus authors create viruses for personal profit. They know how to cover their tracks, and few are ever caught. The viruses have become more sophisticated, less bug-prone, and more precise in delivering a payload. In addition to causing damaging by replicating themselves, the viruses being written today perform functions that range from invasion of privacy to fraud.

Spam advertising is the e-mail equivalent of junk mail. It is often used for large advertising campaigns for questionable products, such as prescription drugs sold without a prescription. Spam advertisers know that there will be a low response rate for their ads, so they want to send it to the widest possible audience. To help perform this task, malicious virus software may commandeer the computers of unsuspecting owners, effectively turning them into robots. The term *botnet* is used to describe an informal network of computers that are acting under the command of controlling software. The computers on the network are described colorfully as *zombie bots* or *drones*. There can be anywhere from a few thousand to hundreds of thousands of zombie bots on a spam botnet. Millions of spam messages can be sent out very quickly by instructing each zombie bot to send spam advertising to everyone in its e-mail contact list. An intelligent spam virus will customize each e-mail message so that it appears to come from the owner of the zombie bot computer. All the while, the owners of the zombie bot computers are completely unaware that this is happening.

Fraud is another reason that professional programmers have entered the virus-writing business. Many viruses steal sensitive personal data from infected computers, including credit card numbers and user names and passwords for online bank accounts. A computer virus can also steal sensitive information by installing spyware in order to track a computer user's keystrokes and mouse clicks.

Spyware installed by viruses is also used for advertising software, known as *adware.* By tracking which Web sites a computer user visits most frequently, adware can target the user's interests. For example, if the user visits Web sites related to health and diet, the seller of a diet plan will pay for pop-up ads for the product to appear on the user's computer.

THE BATTLE AGAINST VIRUSES

As the number of computer viruses multiplied in the late 1980s, researchers began to publish strategies for detecting and eliminating specific viruses. John McAfee (1945–   ) was one of these researchers. He was employed by Lockheed Corporation as a programmer when he received a copy of the Pakistani (c)Brain virus on a floppy disk. This led to an interest in developing software to detect and remove viruses. In 1989, McAfee resigned from Lockheed and founded the antivirus company McAfee Associates, which he initially ran from his Santa Clara home. Other antivirus products, including Norton Anti-Virus from Symantec and Trend Micro Security, were introduced at around the same time. A new industry for antivirus software had been born. Today, all computer owners are advised to purchase and install antivirus software

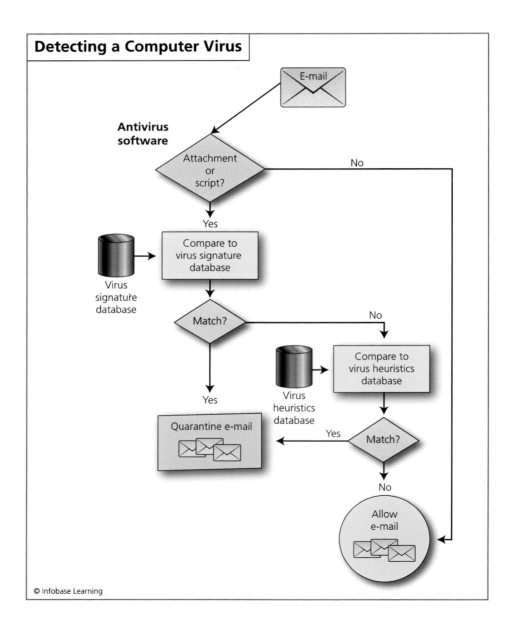

Detecting a Computer Virus

E-mail

Antivirus software

Attachment or script?

No

Yes

Compare to virus signature database

Virus signature database

Match?

No

Yes

Compare to virus heuristics database

Virus heuristics database

Match?

Yes

Quarantine e-mail

No

Allow e-mail

© Infobase Learning

that detects and prevents viruses. In August 2010, the Intel Corporation purchased McAfee for $7.7 billion, which gives some idea of the size of the antivirus software market.

Keeping viruses at bay is a constant battle between virus creators and antivirus software companies and other security professionals. The battle is often described as a high-tech cat-and-mouse game. Every time a new kind of virus is created, security professionals rush to update their antivirus software to protect against the new virus and other ones like it. Virus creators then study the new defenses and attempt to create new viruses that can overcome them.

For antivirus experts employed by software security companies, the first 24 to 48 hours after a new cyber threat is detected can be an adrenaline-inducing time. In August 2010, a reporter for the *Guardian* named Mark King toured Symantec's Dublin facility. His article described the feeling of excitement in the air following the discovery of a new threat and characterized the programmers who track down and break the code of viruses as true detectives, trained in computer forensics and the psychology of malware creators. Patrick Fitzgerald, a member of Symantec's threat intelligence department, described how viruses and worms are detected. "We're constantly monitoring feeds around the Internet, talking to contacts within the industry and using technology to watch out for certain things. Our consumer products also have software that helps us detect attacks as they happen. Hobbyists, who often have as much, or more, knowledge than us, also alert us. We have a 'honeypot' system where we attract malware to come to us, and we monitor Twitter."

(opposite page) Antivirus software uses a variety of techniques to detect viruses on a computer. As this flowchart illustrates, antivirus software may allow e-mail messages that do not contain attachments, scripts, or other code to be opened without further screening because viruses cannot spread through e-mails that contain only plain text. If, however, the e-mail message contains potentially harmful code, the antivirus software compares the code to a database of known viruses. If the code matches a known virus, then the antivirus software places the e-mail message in quarantine so that it cannot do any harm. New viruses, however, will not match any known viruses in the database. Therefore, even e-mail messages that do not contain known viruses are compared against a database of virus heuristics to identify patterns that indicate that the e-mail message might contain a virus. If this step indicates a high probability that the e-mail message contains a virus, then the e-mail is quarantined to avoid the possibility of harm.

In the world of computer security, the bad guys who invent malware are referred to as *black hat hackers,* while security experts who expose malware are known as *white hat hackers.* Once a threat has been detected, the white hats at Symantec and other security companies must quickly come up with a defense against it. This defense is then distributed to customers of the security software in the form of an update.

Individual computer users are the first line of defense in this battle, because it is up to them to make sure they protect their computers from computer viruses and worms. The best antivirus software is useless if it is not installed and run correctly. In corporations and other organizations, IT departments are responsible for guarding against virus invasions. In addition to antivirus software, computers that are connected to the Internet should have a *firewall* installed in order to block unauthorized network access.

Microsoft operating systems and applications have been especially hard-hit by viruses and other malware. Apple Computer has even based advertising campaigns on the claim that their computers are immune to viruses. According to security expert Kevin Haley of Symantec, Microsoft is a big target that has attracted more virus writers. It is expected that as Apple computers continue to become more popular, they too will be subject to malware attacks.

The Microsoft Web site suggests these steps to avoid computer viruses and worms:

- Subscribe to antivirus software and make sure it has the latest virus updates.
- Run with the Microsoft Windows firewall turned on or install an alternative firewall from a reputable company.
- Check for and install Microsoft software updates on a regular basis in order to run with the latest patches to correct system vulnerabilities.
- Avoid opening e-mail attachments from unknown sources. Also avoid opening attachments from friends and acquaintances if the e-mail looks suspicious.
- Use a standard user account rather than an administrator account for day-to-day operations. An administrator account has more access to critical files and functions that can keep a computer from running. A virus that enters through an administrator account is potentially more dangerous.

Robert Tappan Morris, Programmer of an Early Virus

Robert Morris (1965–   ) holds an A.B. (1987) and a Ph.D. (1999) in computer science from Harvard for his work on modeling and controlling networks with large numbers of competing connections. In fall 1988, Morris, then a graduate student at Cornell, began work on a computer program which later became known as the Morris worm. Morris's goal in writing the program was to demonstrate the inadequate security measures on computer networks at the time and show that they could be bypassed relatively easily. By releasing the worm program from one computer connected to the Internet, he intended for it to spread unnoticed to other computers around the country. Morris programmed the worm to spread without detection by not interfering with normal computer operations. He was concerned

(continues)

Robert Tappan Morris, programmer of the Morris Internet worm, which spread much farther and wider than Morris anticipated, causing many computers around the United States to crash or freeze (© *J. L. Atlan/Sygma/Corbis*)

00110101001010011101011010101010101100101000001

(continued)

that multiple copies of the worm on one machine would cause a system crash, so he programmed the worm to check if there was already a copy on the system before installing itself. Morris was concerned that other programmers could kill the worm by writing their own programs that would trick a computer into thinking that the worm was already installed, thereby preventing the true worm from being installed on that computer. In response, Morris programmed the worm to duplicate itself every seventh time that it received a "yes" answer after checking for a copy of itself.

Morris identified four ways for the worm to break into a computer: through a *bug* in a program that transfers and receives e-mail; through a bug in the finger demon program that permits a person to obtain limited information about the computer's user; through a trusted hosts feature that permits a person with certain privileges to have the same privileges on another computer without using a password; and through password guessing, where different combinations of letters are used in the hope that the correct password is eventually guessed, thereby granting to the worm the same level of access to the computer as that of the computer's authorized user.

Morris released the worm from a computer at the Massachusetts Institute of Technology on November 2, 1988, selecting a different university to hide the fact that the worm came from Cornell. However, Morris underestimated the rate of reinfection, which occurred much faster than he anticipated, causing many computers around the country to crash or freeze. The seven to one ratio turned out to be not high enough to slow the program's replication and about 10 percent of ARPANET (the precursor to the Internet) and more than 6,000 computers were affected by the Morris worm. When he realized what had happened, Morris called a friend at Harvard to discuss the situation and try to come up with a way to fix it. Eventually, they decided to send an anonymous message from Harvard

00110101001010011101011010101010101100101000001

CONCLUSIONS

Computer viruses remain a significant threat to the operation of personal and business computers and to the privacy and security of the data on those computers. New viruses are released daily and frequently are used to engage in identity theft and other crimes without detection. As with many biological diseases

`1100111101001010101001100101110110101001010011`

instructing programmers how to kill the worm. Ironically, because the network was clogged as a result of the worm the message did not arrive in time, and computers were affected at many locations, ranging from universities to hospitals to military sites and research facilities. Although the program contained no malicious code and did not erase or damage the computers, the estimated cost of dealing with the worm ranged from $200 to more than $53,000 at each site.

Morris was the first person charged under section 2(d) of the Computer Fraud and Abuse Act of 1986 for the damage caused by his rogue program. He was found guilty following a jury trial, sentenced to 400 hours of community service, a fine of $10,050, and the costs of his supervision. He appealed his conviction to the second circuit, arguing that he lacked intent to cause loss, as required under the act, and that not enough evidence was presented to the jury to conclude that Morris acted "without authorization" as required under the act. The second circuit affirmed the conviction, finding that it was not necessary for the government to prove that the individual intentionally acted to cause loss and that sufficient evidence was presented for the jury to conclude that Morris acted "without authorization" within the meaning of the act.

Morris is currently an associate professor at MIT in the department of electrical engineering and computer science and is affiliated with the Artificial Intelligence Laboratory (CSAIL) in the Parallel and Distributed Operating Systems Group. In 1995, together with Paul Graham, he cofounded Viaweb, the first Web-based application service provider, which was bought by Yahoo! in 1998 and renamed Yahoo! Store. In 2005, again with Paul Graham, he founded a venture capital firm, Y Combinator. Dr. Morris is also a technical adviser to Meraki Networks, a California-based company that provides hardware and software to wireless community networks. In January 2008, he and Paul Graham released a new dialect of the Lisp programming language called Arc.

`1100111101001010101001100101110110101001010011`

for which cures have been found, the technology for keeping viruses at bay has existed for many years. The primary reason, therefore, that viruses continue to spread and do harm is not that security experts do not know how to stop them or that widely available antivirus software is not capable of neutralizing them, but that many owners and operators of computers do not install and maintain antivirus software on their computers diligently enough. Those users who use the latest antivirus software—including high-quality antivirus software that is available freely for download over the Internet—run virtually no risk of infection as long as they avoid engaging in clearly risky Internet behavior. Most virus infections stem from computers that are not sufficiently protected or that are completely unprotected. The topic of computer viruses could largely be relegated to the history books if computer users worldwide would become consistently diligent about taking personal responsibility for ensuring that their own computers were inoculated against infection by computer viruses.

3

SPYWARE: SOFTWARE SNOOPING ON YOUR PRIVATE DATA

Spyware is a broad term that describes software that has been covertly installed on a personal computer to gather information from that computer, such as the user's name, address, and bank account numbers, without the user's knowledge or permission. Spyware may also monitor how a computer is being used, including which Web sites are visited. It may even track keystrokes and mouse clicks, allowing a third party to collect user names and passwords and other personal information. Adware is another type of software that is related to spyware. It is installed on a computer without permission in order to display advertising. Adware usually includes a spyware component that tracks and reports information about the computer user in order to create an advertising profile that can be used to display advertisements that are likely to be attractive to the user.

Although spyware can be used on standalone computers that are not connected to a computer network, the data collected by such spyware cannot easily be provided back to the spyware's creator if that person does not have physical access to the computer being monitored. In contrast, when spyware runs on a computer connected to the Internet, the spyware can easily, quickly, continuously, and surreptitiously transmit any captured data back over the Internet to the creator of the spyware. As a result, the use of spyware has grown alongside growth in the Internet. Any computer that connects to the Internet and accesses even a few Web sites will almost certainly become infected with many pieces of spyware unless that computer is protected by anti-spyware software. This chapter explains how spyware works and how to protect against it.

HOW SPYWARE WORKS

Spyware and adware are typically installed by one of the following methods:

- The computer user installs free software, or *freeware,* that surreptitiously installs spyware. This is most commonly done by file sharing and virus remover freeware.
- The user clicks on a link on a Web page and inadvertently causes the spyware to be installed. This is known in the computer security industry as a *drive-by download.* Instead of displaying a pop-up window that asks the user for permission to install the spyware, the spyware is installed without permission.
- Spyware may be installed by a virus that infects a computer through an e-mail attachment by one of the other virus transport methods.

Once installed, spyware remains in operation until it is removed. The information that is gathered from spyware is relayed to advertisers or other interested parties.

Some free programs that collect computer data notify the user or ask for permission as part of the software's *end-user license agreement (EULA).* For example, the Google toolbar gathers information about how many visitors an individual webpage receives in order to display a PageRank on the toolbar each time the webpage is visited. The data used to determine PageRank is obtained by monitoring the Web browsing habits of users of the toolbar. When a computer user installs the toolbar, he or she is notified that this tracking will take place and can choose not to allow information about Web browsing to be tracked and communicated to Google. Despite the Google toolbar's EULA warning, many people still consider it spyware. Furthermore, many users do not read or understand the entire EULA and may therefore not realize that by installing the Google toolbar they are agreeing to have their Web browsing behavior monitored and transmitted back to Google.

A *cookie* is a text file placed on a computer's hard drive by a Web browser. It stores information that is related to actions taken on a Web page. For example, when the contents of a shopping cart are remembered between Internet sessions, this is probably because they were stored in a cookie. There is a common misconception that all cookies are related to spyware, but this is not the case. Many

How Spyware Works

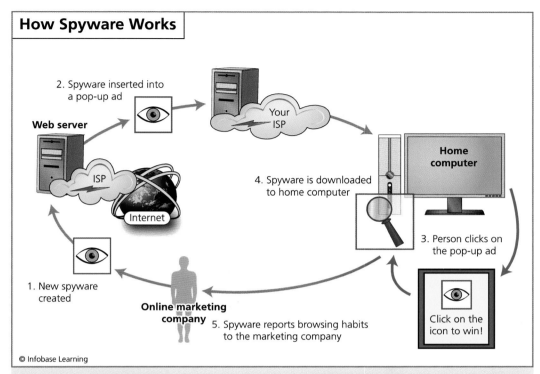

2. Spyware inserted into a pop-up ad

Web server

Your ISP

ISP

Internet

Home computer

4. Spyware is downloaded to home computer

3. Person clicks on the pop-up ad

1. New spyware created

Online marketing company

5. Spyware reports browsing habits to the marketing company

Click on the icon to win!

© Infobase Learning

Spyware secretly tracks a user's computer activity and transmits records of that activity over the Internet to a third party; it often spreads through pop-up advertisements and other content on Web pages. If a user clicks on a pop-up advertisement displayed by a Web browser, the spyware is automatically downloaded and installed onto the user's computer, often without the user's knowledge or full understanding of the purpose of the spyware. The spyware then runs continuously and reports back information about the user, such as the Web sites visited by the user, to a marketing company or other third party, which may use that information to target advertising at the user or to steal the user's identity.

legitimate applications and Web sites use cookies. This confusion about the safety of cookies is part of the general confusion about what constitutes spyware. It can be difficult even for sophisticated computer users, however, to distinguish between useful and harmful cookies. As a result, many users choose to configure their anti-spyware software to err on the side of caution by deleting any cookies that might even possibly be used as spyware. Although automatically deleting such cookies may deprive such users of some benefits of using certain Web sites (such as the ability to have the contents of a shopping cart remembered from one visit to the next), many users consider this to be an acceptable price to pay for additional security and peace of mind.

Web Cookie

Add/Edit Cookie ☒

Name:	level11_authorized
Content:	no
Host:	www.hackthissite.org
Path:	/missions/basic/11/

Send for: ● Any type of connection ○ Encrypted connections only

Expires: ● Expire at end of session
○ New expiration date:

Save Close

© Infobase Learning

A Web cookie is a set of information, stored by a Web browser, associated with a particular Web site visited by a user. One of the earliest uses of cookies was to record the contents of a user's shopping cart at an e-commerce Web site, even if the user did not have an account with that site. Cookies can be used for other purposes, such as storing user names, previously visited webpages, and user preferences.

Spyware can be hazardous since its purpose can include fraud and identity theft. For example, spyware might track a user's passwords as they are typed and then transmit those passwords back to the spyware's creator over the Internet. Such stolen passwords may be used to log into the user's online accounts, including bank accounts, and thereby impersonate the user online and even to steal money directly from the user. Even when spyware is relatively benign, most people dislike the idea of software that tracks how they use their computers. The desire to detect and remove spyware has led to the emergence of an anti-spyware software industry, and running anti-spyware software in addition to antivirus software has become a standard practice among individual computer users and companies. Most Internet security software available today includes both antivirus and anti-spyware features within a single program.

EXAMPLES OF SPYWARE

One of the most famous examples of spyware was Xupiter, an Internet Explorer toolbar that behaved like a *browser hijacker,* replacing a user's home page and redirecting Internet searches to the Xupiter Web site. It also launched pop-up ads (many of which contained offensive adult content) that appeared when the computer user surfed the Internet. The Xupiter spyware was installed as a drive-by download in the early 2000s when many users who ran with low-security browser settings visited Xupiter.com or other deceptive Web sites. Once installed on a computer, the Xupiter spyware was difficult to remove. Following widespread complaints about Xupiter, in 2006 the company that created and distributed it was dissolved.

A more sensational example of spyware was the attempted robbery of Japan's Sumitomo Mitsui bank in 2004. If it had been successful, the robbery would have netted more than $200 million, making it the largest in banking history. The attempted theft began when Kevin O'Donoghue, a security supervisor in the London branch of the bank, allowed Belgian software specialists Jan Van Osselaer and Gilles Poelvoorde to install keylogging spyware on bank computers in order to record account numbers and passwords. Van Osselaer and Poelvoorde then attempted to use this information to transfer money from large accounts. Bank employees noticed that their computers had been tampered with, and the police were informed. The would-be thieves were identified when they filled out electronic transfer forms incorrectly. The three men were apprehended and sentenced to prison terms that varied from three to five years.

Actiance, Inc. (formerly known as FaceTime Communications) produces software that helps businesses control the use of social networks such as Facebook and Twitter by employees. The company maintains a Web site called SpywareGuide.com that tracks and categorizes different types of spyware. In addition to adware, some of the malicious and nonmalicious categories listed by SpywareGuide include:

- *Loyaltyware.* Software that rewards customer loyalty by awarding points, airline miles, or some other prize to shoppers who make purchases from targeted Web sites.
- *Data Miner.* Software that gathers information about a computer user.

(continues on page 38)

Spyware in the Workplace

Employers have always been interested in the productivity of their workers. Employee compensation is usually one of the highest expenses for a business owner, so employers want to be sure that employees are as productive as possible. The widespread use of computers in the workplace has helped increase employee efficiency, but it has also introduced a potential productivity drain, in the form of employees who waste time by browsing the Web, sending and reading personal e-mail, or shopping online. To address this problem, many employers have turned to computer security tools that monitor their employees' computer use.

Most employees are unaware that the contents of their work computer's hard drive can be remotely scanned or that screen shots or keyboard logging can track their online activities and report such activities back to their employers. Employees might consider this type of surveillance to be an invasion of privacy, but employers have the right to monitor the use of their computers, networks, and mobile devices. A recent example of an employer taking action against employees who misused computers at work was the 2008 firing of nine Washington, D.C., city employees who were found to be visiting a large number of pornographic Web sites during work hours. According to the *Washington Post*, a computer-monitoring product called WebSense revealed that each of the fired employees had viewed porn sites more than 19,000 times in the previous year.

Employers may also have reason to track the use of company computers to maintain security of their sensitive data, because computers can be used by employees to access, modify, and steal such data. Since the volume of data that moves across an organization's computer network can be very large, software tools are used to help detect potential threats. One of the most widely used security software products is Guidance Software's EnCase. The primary goal of this software is to analyze digital media to detect hackers, malware, and other threats that can come either from external sources or from company employees. Since employees are familiar with a company's internal operations, they pose the largest risk in terms of attacks on sensitive data. Security software helps automate the surveillance process by detecting suspicious data patterns and analyzing logged events. When suspicious activity is detected, an image of the employee's hard drive or any external drive can be captured and saved for forensic analysis by a security expert. Security software can find data that is currently on a computer's hard drive as well as data that has been deleted. EnCase software has been used

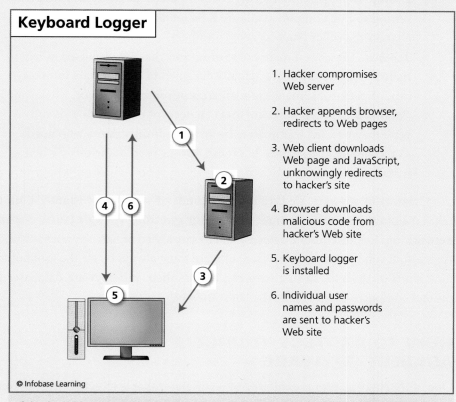

Keyboard Logger

1. Hacker compromises Web server

2. Hacker appends browser, redirects to Web pages

3. Web client downloads Web page and JavaScript, unknowingly redirects to hacker's site

4. Browser downloads malicious code from hacker's Web site

5. Keyboard logger is installed

6. Individual user names and passwords are sent to hacker's Web site

© Infobase Learning

A keyboard logger monitors and records all of the keys pressed by a user on a particular computer, usually without the user's knowledge. This drawing illustrates how a keyboard logger may be automatically downloaded to and installed on a user's computer in response to the user visiting a Web page that has been compromised by a hacker. Once the keyboard logger is installed and running on the user's computer, the keyboard logger may detect the user's usernames and passwords as they are typed and then transmit them back to the hacker over the Internet.

by law enforcement agencies to track down and convict criminals who left evidence of their crimes on their hard drives.

Employers can also use company-owned gadgets to spy on employees when they are out of the office. An employee of the New York City school system who was fired for repeatedly leaving work early took his case to court. His case was dismissed when the school system introduced GPS evidence from his work-issued cellphone that showed he had been leaving work early for several months.

(continued from page 35)

- *Dialup.* A program that changes a computer's dialup connection setting so that computer calls are directed to a phone number which charges the caller (such as a 900 number).
- **Trojans.** These are Trojan horse programs that are disguised as legitimate applications but are actually designed to steal private information or perform some other malicious purpose.
- *Password Cracker.* Software that can decrypt passwords. This software may be used legitimately by system administrators who need to recover lost passwords, but it can also be used maliciously when installed as spyware.

Creators of spyware are creating new kinds of spyware constantly, both to take advantage of new kinds of technology for spreading spyware (such as social networking sites and mobile devices) and to stay ahead of anti-spyware software. As a result, vendors of anti-spyware software must always be on the lookout for new kinds of spyware so that they can update their anti-spyware databases to protect computer users against the latest threats.

HOW TO PROTECT YOURSELF AGAINST SPYWARE

One of the first symptoms exhibited by a computer that is infected with spyware is degradation in performance. The computer's Internet connection may suddenly seem slower or the computer may freeze up more frequently. The process for removing spyware can be difficult (see the following section). To avoid spending time tracking down hidden spyware, every computer user should take a few simple preventative steps to avoid spyware infection.

- *Download with caution*

  Avoid the temptation to download freeware unless you are sure that it is from a reputable source and does not included spyware or adware. Be especially wary of free anti-spyware software. This rogue ware is often spyware in disguise. Research anti-spyware software before downloading or installing it.

- *Read the end-user license agreement*

  The EULA is the legal-sounding text that is displayed and must be agreed to before many software programs are installed. Before agreeing to a

Most antivirus software today has the ability to detect, block, and remove both viruses and spyware. This screenshot of a Norton antivirus product shows an example in which a virus has been detected and automatically removed so that it cannot harm the user's computer. The antivirus software also informs the user (in the details section) that many other users have reported this virus as a high risk. The user can also click on the more links to obtain more details about the virus and to learn about the origin of the virus. *(Symantec Corporation)*

EULA for new software, read it to make sure that the software does not include any features that can be categorized as spyware.

- *Click pop up dialog buttons carefully*
  Some Web sites display pop-up dialogs that contain OK and cancel buttons (or yes and no buttons). Read any message in the pop-up carefully

before clicking on one of the buttons, since the message may be asking whether you grant permission to install software. Even better, install a pop-up blocker or turn on pop-up blocking in your Web browser.

- *Use antivirus software that includes anti-spyware tools*
The most popular antivirus products now also scan for adware and spyware. This includes Norton AntiVirus, McAfee VirusScan, and Trend Micro Internet Security. To keep a personal computer secure, always run with antivirus software enabled and schedule regular scans for spyware and adware.

- *Update often*
Configure your computer security software to update itself with the latest virus and spyware definitions automatically and frequently. Otherwise, your computer may be at risk of being infected by newly developed adware even if your antivirus software is running.

Although no preventative measure can guarantee safety from spyware, following the steps listed above diligently will protect against the most common and dangerous forms of spyware.

WHAT TO DO IF YOUR COMPUTER IS INFECTED

Once a computer has become infected with spyware and adware, it can be difficult to eradicate it. In many cases, the standard computer tools for uninstalling software are ineffective in removing spyware and adware. The following are some suggestions for finding and removing spyware from a computer:

- A computer that shows signs of being seriously infected should be disconnected from the Internet as the first step in repairing it. For example, if pop-up windows are being displayed continuously or computer performance has been compromised, then Internet access should be turned off.
- Try to uninstall spyware and adware using the traditional methods such as Add/Remove Programs in Microsoft Windows. Special uninstaller programs, such as Advanced Uninstaller Pro and Ashampoo Uninstaller, may be more successful at completely uninstalling such software. If the uninstall process completes successfully, reboot the computer.

Spyware Defense

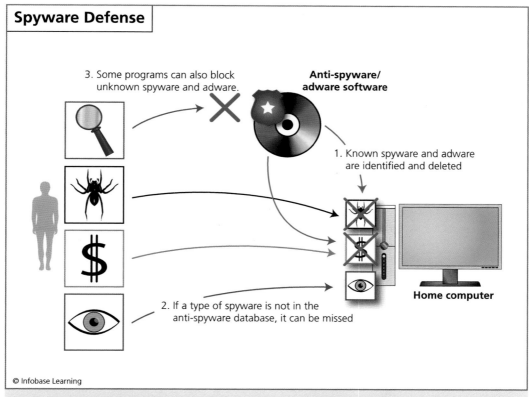

3. Some programs can also block unknown spyware and adware.

Anti-spyware/ adware software

1. Known spyware and adware are identified and deleted

Home computer

2. If a type of spyware is not in the anti-spyware database, it can be missed

© Infobase Learning

Anti-spyware and anti-adware software, known generally as anti-malware software, typically contains a database of known spyware and adware. This enables the anti-malware software to compare any new software downloaded onto a computer against the database to determine whether such new software is known spyware or adware. Any such known spyware or adware that is detected can be deleted or blocked from running. New spyware or adware that is not in the database, however, may pass by undetected. As a result, some anti-malware software looks for clues that software downloaded onto the computer is spyware or adware, even if the downloaded software is not an exact match for spyware or adware in the database.

- If the uninstall process worked and the computer has been rebooted successfully, run a full system scan with antivirus software. Although this may take longer than running a typical quick scan, the full system scan will check for any remaining traces of the spyware or adware that was removed.

- If you suspect that your computer has been invaded by malicious spyware that cannot be removed using traditional methods, seek

(continues on page 44)

0011010100101001101011010101010101100101000001

Steve Gibson, Founder of Gibson Research Corporation

Born in 1955 in Dayton, Ohio, Steve Gibson has been fascinated by computers and electronics from an early age, working on projects as early as four years old. At 15, while still in high school, he worked in the Artificial Intelligence Laboratory at Stanford University alongside Stanford's postgraduate students, participating in projects that included the world's first functioning laser printer, machine learning, and prototype Mars and Venus probes. Also while in high school, Steve developed and taught two years of computer science electronics curriculum, which is still being taught throughout the San Mateo Union high school district. Gibson graduated from the University of California, Berkeley, with a degree in electrical engineering and computer science and a 4.0 GPA. In 1978, at the age of 23, Steve founded Gibson and Garnish Advertising, a firm that specialized in media advertisement and public relations for high-tech computer and related firms. The promising young firm was purchased by a major advertising agency within six months of opening.

At the age of 26, Gibson founded Gibson Laboratories, Inc., a hardware and software manufacturing firm that designed and developed a light pen system pointing device (a computerized pen that can be used instead of a mouse, touch screen, or tablet) for Apple II home computers. Gibson Labs was bought by Atari Corporation, which wanted to develop the technology further. Gibson was able to recover all rights to proprietary hardware and software after subsequent management reorganization at Atari and manufactured a successor product, Gibson Light Pen for Apple II computers, through Koala Technologies.

From 1983 to 1985, Gibson was a contributing editor to *InfoWorld* magazine, writing about research and developments in computer software and technology. Gibson's extensive knowledge of computer software and hardware and experience in the field made his opinion particularly valuable to the magazine readers. He continues to publish articles in *InfoWorld* as a contributing editor and writer of the TechTalk column.

Gibson next began working on improving the color graphics adapter display (CGA) of new IBM personal computers. Due to hardware limitations, the screens noticeably flickered when scrolling. Gibson created a software program called FlickerFree that eliminated the problem and increased display speed and, in 1985, incorporated Gibson Research Corporation, a software development firm. Gibson

0011010100101001101011010101010101100101000001

Steve Gibson, founder of computer security and software firm Gibson Research Corporation, shown here in his home office in Laguna Hills, California *(AP Images)*

is the sole shareholder of GRC and is primarily responsible for the research and development of GRC's products. Over the years, GRC has released ChromaZone, the first 3D virtual reality real-time interactive screen saver set, which received high praise from industry magazines and was awarded Dr. File Finder's Pick for December 1995 on Microsoft Network. GRC is also responsible for SpinRite, a hard-drive reformatting utility for IBM PC, which prevents damage to the hard drive resulting from wear and tear over the years. OptOut, another GRC product, was one of the first adware removal programs.

In the 1990s, Gibson began to focus on computer security and has released numerous security tools. Amongst these is ShieldsUp!, a device that scans for any ports opened through a user's firewall and alerts for potential attempted unauthorized access to one's computer. Gibson is currently working on DNS Benchmark, a freeware DNS performance and security utility. In April 2009, Gibson announced that DNSbench is almost complete and should be ready soon for distribution.

Together with Leo Laporte, Gibson cohosts a weekly computer security podcast called *Security Now!* He is also a frequent guest on Laporte's technology podcast *This Week in Tech*. Gibson lives in Laguna Hills, California.

(continued from page 41)

the help of a computer security specialist. After the specialist has removed the spyware, minimize the residual damage by changing passwords to sensitive data, such as passwords for bank accounts and credit cards.

- If a computer's e-mail account has been used to spread spyware or adware, an e-mail message should be sent to all contacts in the address book to let them know that they may be in danger of infection and to watch for suspicious e-mail messages from the same e-mail address. Consider deactivating the e-mail address and obtaining a new e-mail address for future use.
- Check credit card statements for unauthorized charges and report them to credit card companies. Report your credit cards as lost or stolen to get cards with new numbers, just in case. Sign up for a credit-monitoring service for a few months to be on the lookout for suspicious activity.
- To avoid future infection by spyware and adware, exercise caution when downloading free software. Set your Web browser security levels to medium or high and install the most current operating system updates.

The best way to avoid having to remove spyware and adware is to use the latest anti-malware software to protect against infection. If, however, a computer is infected, the steps above typically are successful at removing malware without the need to completely uninstall and reinstall the computer's operating system from scratch.

CONCLUSIONS

Spyware has become both more prominent and more dangerous in response to the increasingly common use of computers to store and share personal information. Unlike viruses that seek to damage data on computers or to hijack such computers to engage in criminal activity, spyware attempts to leave the computers it infects as unharmed as possible, to minimize the likelihood that the spyware will be detected as it silently monitors information stored on, transmitted by, and downloaded to those computers. Spyware grows more valuable over time to those who use it to gather personal information from others, because a single piece of spyware installed on a computer can continue to intercept and transmit information about the computer's owner for as long as the spyware remains unnoticed.

It can be challenging to protect oneself against spyware. Reverting to use of paper and ink to store sensitive information is not a practical option for most people. Although encrypting data stored on a computer can reduce the likelihood that such data will be accessible to spyware, the computer's user typically must decrypt that information at some point to use it, as in the case of a password that must be decrypted so that it can be used to log in to a Web site. Spyware that monitors passwords typed into Web browsers will detect such passwords as they are typed in their unencrypted form. Some Web sites attempt to neutralize such spyware by requiring passwords to be entered by clicking buttons on on-screen keyboards, which can be difficult or impossible for spyware to track, especially if the layout of such keyboards changes each time they are displayed. Another relatively effective way to mitigate the effectiveness of spyware is to change passwords frequently or to use the one-time passwords that are being issued increasingly frequently by credit card companies, e-commerce Web sites, and other entities.

As in the case of viruses, it will probably never be possible for computer users to rely on technological solutions alone to combat spyware. Instead, users will need to employ a combination of defensive technology (such as anti-spyware software), good habits (such as changing passwords frequently), and common sense (such as not entering passwords on public computers) to protect themselves against becoming the victims of spyware.

4

PHISHING AND SOCIAL ENGINEERING: CONFIDENCE GAMES GO ONLINE

This chapter explains how *phishing* schemes—such as e-mails asking the user to confirm his or her bank account number and PIN—work, how they are used to invade people's privacy, and how to protect oneself against them.

CONFIDENCE GAMES: THE PREHISTORY OF PHISHING

The first use of the term *confidence man—con man,* for short—dates to 1849, when a smartly dressed William Thompson would approach a *mark* on the streets of New York City and pretend that they were old friends. After gaining the mark's trust, Thompson would ask to borrow the man's watch for a day. Since a scheme of this fashion requires the mark's confidence, *grifters* came to be called confidence men.

Typically, confidence games take advantage of human nature. Most people can be manipulated through greed, vanity, or compassion. Naïve victims may trust the con artist to deliver on promises or good faith gestures. One of the most famous confidence games is the devastating *Ponzi scheme.* The con artist running a Ponzi scheme will take investment capital from marks, offering a large return on their investment. Instead of investing the money, the con artist simply fabricates records of investments and profits. As long as the profits appear to be legitimate, most of the marks will not ask for their money back. Those who do can be paid, at first, with money that has been invested by other marks. Since the

Ponzi Scheme

1 participant
To get paid
takes 14 participants

2 participants
For all to get paid at this
level takes 28 participants

4 participants
For all to get paid at this
level takes 56 participants

8 participants
For all to get paid at this
level takes 112 participants

32 participants
For all to get paid at this level takes 448 participants

256 participants
For all to get paid at this level takes 3,584 participants

512 participants
For all to get paid at this level takes 7,168 participants

1,024 participants
For all to get paid at this level takes 14,336 participants

© Infobase Learning

An illustration of a Ponzi-type pyramid scheme that shows that as the number of participants in the scheme grows, the number of additional participants required to pay back
the initial investment of earlier participants grows exponentially. Although a pyramid
scheme can pay back its original investors as long as the total number of investors grows
sufficiently quickly, eventually it becomes impossible to recruit new investors quickly
enough, at which point the entire system collapses, causing any investors who have not
already received a full return on their investment to lose all of the money they put into
the system. As a result, all pyramid schemes eventually cause the most recent, largest
group of investors to lose their entire investment. Despite this fact, Ponzi schemes remain
alluring to unsophisticated investors because they can provide very large returns on
investment very quickly for early investors.

scheme shows large returns, and most investors have no problem withdrawing their money from the con, marks serve as unwitting shills when they tell their friends about the success they are having. Though the first Ponzi scheme was named for Charles Ponzi, who stole millions from investors in the 1920s, the most recent infamous Ponzi scheme was orchestrated by Bernard Madoff, who stole upward of $65 billion. Both Ponzi and Madoff were convicted of investment fraud and served time in prison.

Other types of confidence games, like the Nigerian scam, affect people and businesses. In the most common Nigerian scam, letters or e-mails are sent to marks promising rewards. The trickster only needs the mark to pay a processing fee, bribe, or some other paltry sum in order to receive a great windfall. In another variation, growing more popular with the increased activity on online auction sites such as eBay or online classified ad sites, such as Craigslist, the scammer will send a fake cashier's check to be deposited at the mark's bank. After the mark notifies the con man that the check has been deposited, the mark will

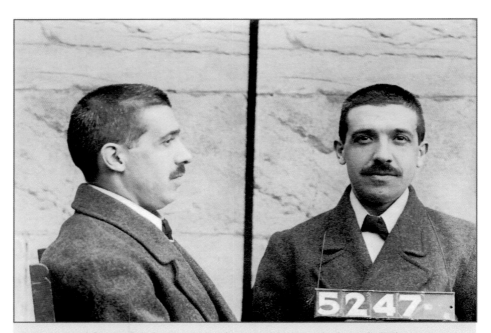

Mug shots of Charles Ponzi, perpetrator of a pyramid scheme in the early 20th century. This particular type of fraud has been referred to ever since as a Ponzi scheme. *(© Bettmann/CORBIS)*

be asked to wire back part or all of the funds. The bank, unaware that the check is fraudulent, will accept the payment and increase the account balance, only to reverse the transaction when the cashier's check bounces, holding the victim responsible. Any money wired to the scammer in the meantime will be gone forever. The Nigerian scam has been devastating to both individual marks and businesses. In 2010, two Honolulu law firms lost a combined total of $500,000 in sophisticated Nigerian scams.

SOCIAL ENGINEERING

Modern confidence games can be more subtle. For instance, a social engineer might call a computer administrator and pretend to be a consultant. By simply asking for sensitive information, like user names or passwords, or by instructing the administrator to type certain commands into a terminal, the administrator might divulge enough information for a hacker to gain entry without time-consuming brute force attacks.

Social engineering refers to any kind of confidence game where individuals are manipulated into divulging information, performing actions, or making errors that allow a social engineer to gather information, commit fraud, or gain access to a computer system.

THE TECHNOLOGY OF PHISHING

Phishing refers to the malicious creation of Web sites and e-mails that pose as legitimate but in reality are merely tools for collecting one's financial and personal information. A phishing e-mail may introduce the writer as a security analyst, asking the user to confirm a password, date of birth, Social Security number, or other piece of information. When the user clicks send on a reply, he or she will be sending personal information to someone who has no affiliation with the legitimate business and could misuse the information.

Phishing can also be accomplished by link manipulation. *Hyperlinks* have two properties, the text of the hyperlink and the URL the hyperlink redirects to. By making the hyperlink appear legitimate, but changing the URL to an identical, but malicious, Web site, victims will often enter login credentials, account information, or personal data.

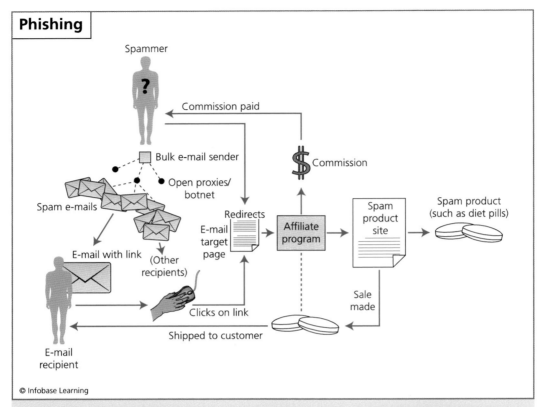

Phishing

Spammer

Commission paid

Bulk e-mail sender

Commission

Open proxies/botnet

Spam e-mails

Redirects

Spam product site

Spam product (such as diet pills)

E-mail target page

Affiliate program

E-mail with link

(Other recipients)

Sale made

Clicks on link

E-mail recipient

Shipped to customer

© Infobase Learning

Phishing schemes often spread using spam e-mail messages. A spammer embeds a phishing lure within an e-mail message and sends the message to thousands of recipients. For example, the lure might be a link that appears to point to a legitimate e-commerce Web site (such as Amazon) but which instead points to a spam product site (such as a site that sells diet pills). Anyone who opens the message and is tricked into clicking on the phishing link is redirected to the spam-product site instead of the legitimate site. The spammer is automatically paid a commission by the spam product site in exchange for luring the user. If the user then purchases a product from the spam product site, the owner of that site receives revenue from the user for only the small cost of paying the commission to the spammer.

As users become more computer-savvy, phishers are forced to target newer devices like mobile phones. Scamming users via text is becoming more common. Following the massive success of Apple's mobile products, phishing e-mails appearing to be receipts for expensive purchases from Apple's App Store convince users to investigate further by clicking on a link and entering their App Store user name and password into a malicious Web site.

Social networks open new possibilities of scarily efficient phishing. After gaining access to a victim's account information, phishers can encourage the victim's friends to click phishing links, creating a pyramid of unsecure accounts. Scammers often use these phished accounts to prey on victims of a *London scam*. Once a scammer has access to a trusted friend's account, the scammer, posing as a friend, will explain that he or she is stranded in London with no way of getting home. The victim will be asked to wire money to help the friend get home. Experiments have shown that while traditional phishing dupes about 16 percent of respondents social phishing dupes a whopping 72 percent.

PROMINENT PHISHING SCAMS

The term *phishing* originated in the mid-1990s. At the time, it was possible to use randomly generated credit card numbers to set up AOL accounts, a loophole that AOL caught and closed in 1995. The people who used these randomly generated numbers to set up fraudulent accounts (typically members of the *warez* community, traders of pirated software) began phishing for real accounts, sending instant messages to AOL members asking them to provide their password or reveal account information. Once they had the victim's password, they could use the victim's account to send or receive pirated software.

Phishing examples include the following:

- A social engineer pretending to be a confused and befuddled person will call a clerk and meekly request a password change. If the clerk is duped, the hacker will have the user's password.
- Seemingly powerful and hurried people, identifying themselves as executives, will telephone a new system administrator and demand access to their account. If the administrator is intimidated or if he feels his job is threatened, he could reveal log-in credentials to the social engineer. At an airport, hackers will look over users' shoulders *(shoulder surfing)* as telephone, credit card numbers, or ATM PINs (sometimes even using binoculars or camcorders) are keyed.
- A hacker will call and confidently instruct a computer operator to type in a few lines of instruction at the console, enabling the hacker to gain access to the system.
- An attacker will sift through paper trash (also known as *dumpster diving*), looking for clues to unlock IT treasures or financial information.

The Nigerian Scam

A Nigerian scam, also known as a 419 scam or advance fee fraud, is a scam involving a wealthy foreigner who needs assistance in moving millions of dollars from his home country, promising a large reward in exchange for helping him.

It became an extremely popular scam in the late '90s, when e-mails could be mass-mailed to droves of inexperienced computer users. Typically, a Nigerian scam e-mail looks similar to this:

Dear Sir or Madam:

I am Mr. Mark David, a wealthy Nigerian prince. Due to the recent military conflict in my country, I am unable to withdraw any of my money from the First Bank of Nigeria. The money totals an amount of $14 million and, if you pay the $1,000 bank wire fee required for moving the money to an American bank, you will be rewarded with a sum of $2 million. I look forward to your earliest reply.

Yours,
Mr. Mark David

Some readers, blinded by the promise of a large windfall, will agree to pay the small fee. After the money is transferred, the scammer will either disappear or string the victim along with more requests for money.

In a more sophisticated version of the scam, using letterhead from a major company, a scammer will enter into a lucrative business relationship with a firm. A contract will be drafted and signed with concessions from the victim, usually an up-front payment of associated fees. At this point, the scammer either will disappear with the victim's money or, if the victim believes the business deal is lucrative enough, he might be convinced to send additional funds.

The number 419 refers to the Nigerian penal statute dealing with fraud.

Phishing can also be done by phone, where a recorded message, allegedly from a bank, is left on a customer's voice mail with instructions and a number to call back. The message routes callers to an automated system, where they are asked to enter their account numbers and personal identification numbers (PINs).

The Nigerian scam, also known as the Nigerian letter, the 419 fraud, the Nigerian bank scam, and the Nigerian money offer, is one of the most common frauds perpetrated over the Internet. It usually takes the form of an e-mail message sent to millions of people that claims to have been sent by a Nigerian government official or bank employee to just one recipient. The sender claims to know of a large amount of money that he cannot access, but that could be obtained with the help of the recipient of the e-mail message. Although the precise details of the scam vary widely, the sender typically promises the recipient a large percentage of the money in exchange for providing assistance in obtaining it. The sender attempts to convince the recipient to provide a loan or pay other fees to assist in the process of obtaining the promised cash. Recipients who are convinced by the scammer then provide money over the Internet, but of course are never provided with any of the promised funds in return. This photograph shows signs in an Internet café in Nigeria, warning computer users there against sending such fraudulent e-mails. *(AP Images)*

HOW TO PROTECT AGAINST PHISHING

Technology can rarely stop a phishing attack. Since social engineering involves mistakes made by humans, not flaws in computer security, there is no firewall

(continues on page 56)

Kevin Mitnick, Computer Security Consultant, Reformed Hacker

Born in 1963, Mitnick is the founder of Mitnick Security Consulting, LLP, which provides security assessments and advice to businesses. Mitnick is also the author of two books on computer security, *The Art of Intrusion,* which focuses on real stories of security breaches, and *The Art of Deception,* which details social engineering as a means of obtaining security information.

Kevin Mitnick, convicted computer hacker and now paid computer security consultant *(© Jurgen Frank/ Corbis Outline)*

His first brush with law enforcement resulted in his being placed on probation for stealing computer manuals from a Los Angeles telephone switching center. However, he became famous as a result of publicity following his break-in to the North American Air Defense Command computer in 1982 and his gaining control of telephone company switching centers in Manhattan and all of California. Mitnick was caught in 1988 after he secretly read e-mails of computer security officials at MCI Communications that allowed him to learn how the company computers and phones were protected. It is estimated that he had caused $4 million worth of damage and stolen $1 million worth of software. He was sentenced to a year in a low-security federal prison in California. In July 1989, after being released from prison where he spent a year in solitary confinement, Mitnick was placed in a treatment program to treat his addiction to computers and spent six months without touching a computer modem. Mitnick, however, continued to hack, eventually breaking into computers at Pacific Bell.

Mitnick achieved notoriety when, after a warrant was issued for his arrest, he fled the state. During his two-and-a-half years as a fugitive, Mitnick broke into numerous computer networks, broke many of the protections on Motorola, NEC, and Nokia cellular phones, read confidential corporate e-mails, and wiretapped the California DMV. According to Mitnick, he was never motivated by personal gain and just wanted to "become better at getting in."

After Mitnick pled guilty to his crimes, he was sent to prison for five years. He was released in 2000. Upon his release from prison, Mitnick's terms of probation prohibited him from using the tools he had previously used to commit his crimes, namely phones and computers, as well as from accepting employment in computer and telecommunications industries, because the court concluded that he would be unlikely to use these devices in a legal manner. With few job prospects after his release, Mitnick was invited by Democratic senator Joe Lieberman and Republican Fred Thompson to speak before their panel on how government's computer security could be improved. This engaging presentation was very successful and was followed by invitations for speaking engagements all over the country, including appearances on local and national network programs, *60 Minutes, Court TV, Good Morning America,* and a guest starring role on ABC's spy drama *Alias.* Mitnick did not begin using the Web until 2003, when his probation expired.

According to Mitnick, the weakest link in a secure environment is the person holding the key. Mitnick admitted to using a number of social engineering confidence tricks in order to gain access to computer networks. When Mitnick was 17 years old, he went to a telecommunication company's central office and convinced the guard on duty that he was there to collect old ID cards before new ones were delivered. The guard gave Mitnick his ID card. In order to get the company's complete telephone directory, including unlisted numbers, Mitnick called the company office and told them to leave the directory outside their door, because he needed to collect and shred it before delivering the new directory.

Mitnick's hacking skills are now in demand as a security consultant. He is the founder of Mitnick Security Consulting, LLP, which provides security assessments and advice to various businesses. Today, Mitnick warns his clients about the dangers of identity theft, something that as a former hacker he knows very well. The danger of having personal information compromised is that it can be used again and again without the victim's knowledge. Armed with a Social Security number,

(continues)

001101010010100111010110101010101011001010001

(continued)

a hacker can even file a tax return and collect a refund, something that the IRS is not well-prepared to handle. In addition to recommending physically securing information, Mitnick's main message is that the most important step in protecting information is being vigilant and not disclosing data to someone who may pose as someone legitimately needing that information, such as a bank representative. Social engineering, as this method is known, is in fact the very same way in which Mitnick collected the bulk of his information while he was a hacker.

001101010010100111010110101010101011001010001

(continued from page 53)

that effectively stops attempts at phishing. Some antivirus software or firewalls can be marginally useful at detecting malicious phishing Web sites, but a sophisticated attack aimed at a particular user or organization will always avoid detection by any software application.

People can avoid most phishing by being very careful about disclosing personal information. Always verify that a Web site is genuine (check the URL bar) before entering a password. A genuine Web site will typically use the organization's official Web domain (e.g., chase.com) instead of a phony domain. If contacted by an employee of a bank or another third party, like a consulting firm, always get a name and extension, and then call the company back at the number listed in the telephone book. Don't type in passwords, ATM pins, or credit card numbers with anyone standing nearby. Above all, never fall victim to scare tactics, pressure, or threats from a phisher.

The fight against phishing has encouraged all Web browsers to prominently display a lock icon in the corner of the screen when using secure Web sites. The icon appears unlocked when the Web site does not require the use of *SSL (Secure Sockets Layer)* encryption, a giveaway for many phishing sites. Many popular Web browsers have begun using software such as McAfee SiteAdvisor to actively alert users to malicious Web sites as well.

Two-factor authentication, like a password and *RSA* authenticator, can prevent hackers from accessing a victim's account even if they obtain the password. An RSA authenticator will display a string of random numbers that changes every minute or two. Only the user holding the authenticator will be able to access the account.

CONCLUSIONS

In one sense, there is nothing new about phishing. It is merely the application of age-old confidence games to the Internet. However, phishing is particularly dangerous because it leverages several features of online communication to increase the likelihood that the targets will bite. First, phishing artists take advantage of the apparent intimacy of online communication, such as e-mail and text messaging, to quickly forge what appears to the recipient to be a close personal bond. Second, the text-based nature of the communications mechanisms used by most phishing artists makes it impossible for those who receive phishing messages to rely on body language, tone of voice, and other physical cues to draw conclusions about the legitimacy of the phishing request. Third, the difficulty of tracking down phishing artists online tends to embolden them to target larger numbers of people more frequently than they would be likely to do if they were limited to approaching pedestrians on the sidewalk. Fourth, the ease of copying legitimate e-mail messages and Web sites to create what appear to be official messages from banks, credit card companies, e-tailers, and employers makes it difficult for even sophisticated computer users to distinguish forgeries from originals. Finally, the ability to hide phony links underneath legitimate text (such as by making the text "Bank of America" link to a phishing site instead of to the real Bank of America Web site) increases the likelihood that computer users, having become accustomed to clicking quickly on links without pausing first to investigate them, will be deceived by electronic messages in ways that would not be possible with messages sent by postal mail or made in person.

Although some technological advances have been made recently in the battle against phishing, confidence games succeed primarily as a result of social factors, not technological flaws. As a result, the primary defense against phishing will likely be to educate Internet users about how phishing schemes work, the warning signs of a phishing attack, and the steps to take in the event that one realizes that one has taken the bait of a phishing scheme. Although this may ultimately require users to sacrifice a bit of what they value most on the Internet— the ability to race quickly from message to message and from link to link—by pausing to reflect for just a moment before every keystroke and click, the gains in personal security should convince most Internet users that the tradeoff is a worthwhile one.

5

YOUR PERSONAL INFORMATION ONLINE: EVERYONE IS A PUBLIC FIGURE NOW

This chapter discusses the benefits and costs of the huge repository of information that is the Internet. This chapter will explain the risks to privacy and security of providing personal information online—such as on Facebook pages and blogs—and how to make responsible decisions about providing such information.

THE PERMANENCE OF ONLINE RECORDS

Creating a permanent record of all human knowledge has long been a dream of technologists. In 1945, Vannevar Bush, in an article in the *Atlantic Monthly,* described an electromechanical device that an individual could use to store notes created by that individual. The device, dubbed a *memex* (an abbreviation for memory index), would be a sort of personal library. In Bush's paper, he described a means for the memex to link to notes recorded by other researchers. Though Bush likely did not picture these links as underlined and blue, this vision is credited as the inspiration for the hypertext systems that predated the Internet.

As personal, portable libraries, computers are a huge repository of knowledge, any of which can be called upon with no more than a few keystrokes typed into a *search engine.* Online versions of reference materials, such as newspaper articles, court decisions, and historical documents, allow extensive research to be performed in a fraction of the time required when using their paper and ink predecessors. Moreover, computers have made

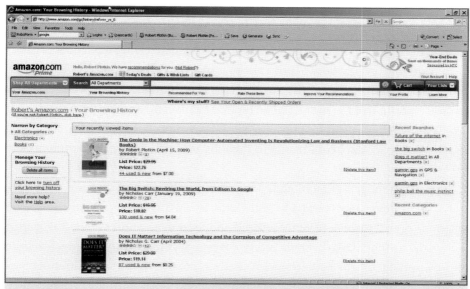

Although many Web users are aware that e-commerce sites record which products they have purchased, many are not aware that records are kept of the products they view but do not purchase. This screenshot shows books that a computer user has viewed but not purchased on Amazon. The Web site may use this information for purposes such as deciding which similar books to recommend to the same user in the future. *(Robert Plotkin)*

this information accessible to people who could not afford to purchase them or travel to the specialized libraries and repositories where they were located.

The cost of this interconnected and permanent set of online records can be steep. Slanderous, embarrassing, and otherwise hurtful information never goes away, no matter how untrue it may be. Celebrities are regularly at the mercy of online tabloids. Politicians increasingly find themselves criticized for statements they made or votes they cast 30 or 40 years ago, when the culture was far different than it is today. Once such statements are published online, there is virtually no way to remove them.

Just as consumers favor e-commerce sites to find products more easily, the owners of e-commerce sites use their customers' purchasing and browsing histories to identify additional products and services to market to those customers. Although most online consumers are aware that their actual purchases are tracked by e-tailers, many are not aware that the products they view and the searches they type are also stored, even if such activity does not result in purchases. Even the amount of time that a user spends viewing a particular product's page may be tracked. All of this information is then used to identify the user's likes and dislikes and thereby to make recommendations for the user and to create a profile of the user that can be sold to advertising companies and other e-tailers. Although most e-tailers enable users to turn such tracking off, at least in part, doing so can be difficult and must be repeated at each e-commerce site separately.

E-mail messages, often intended as extemporaneous and personal conversations, live forever in cyberspace. Bill Gates learned this very expensive lesson when his e-mail records were uncovered and used in an antitrust lawsuit against Microsoft in the 1990s. E-mails are typically not intended by those who write and transmit them to be permanent. Rather, most e-mails are written as part of communications that the sender and recipient both think of as temporary, informal conversations. There is a sharp contrast, therefore, between the actual permanence of such communications online and their intended transience.

Ironically, although the permanence of digital information is intended to facilitate the process of finding desired information quickly, in practice information permanence can make certain information more difficult to locate. For example, tools such as Google Desktop can search through everything stored on a hard drive, including word processing documents, e-mail messages, Adobe Acrobat (PDF) documents, and more. Such search technology draws no distinction between information that was meant to persist and information that was meant to be temporary. As a result, the search is likely to produce trivial results that obscure the truly important pieces of information that the user was trying to find. Everyone has had the same experience when searching the Web for a nugget of information, only to obtain thousands of irrelevant hits. Although one way to reduce this problem would be for users and Web site owners to delete information after it loses relevance, it is not practical to expect people to spend the time necessary to sift through old information to separate the relevant from the irrelevant. Although some experts have suggested tackling this problem using technological innovations, such as electronic data fading (which would automatically delete information after it loses relevance), such technology has not yet become reliable enough to use.

OFFLINE RECORDS GO ONLINE

Digital conversion of archived material has advanced rapidly in recent years. *Digitization* is now possible for nearly every medium and format of information presently contained in libraries, records rooms, and archives, from musical recordings to manuscripts. The advent of automatic scanning hardware and software plus the invention and propagation of database technology is creating virtual libraries of information all over the Web. Judges, lawmakers, and those responsible for policy matters often struggle to understand new technologies and, more important, to grasp the implications of those technologies and to understand what the digitization of archives means for the public.

Digitization often reduces costs, promises benefits, and creates a more efficient way to store and retrieve information. Yet digitization can also create problems, even when placing information online that was previously available offline to the public for free. If information is already publicly available offline, it might at first glance seem logical that simply placing such information online would not raise any additional privacy or security questions. This is rarely the case, however, due to the easy, instant, free, and global nature of access to information online.

One of the most valuable qualities of digital information is that it is not fixed in the way that printed material is. Digital information remains fluid until it is printed, for it can be changed easily and without trace. Although this flexibility is in one sense an improvement over paper-based storage, it complicates things considerably from the perspective of archives that seek to maintain records that are both final and definitive.

From a technological perspective, the digital medium also suffers from complex issues in data preservation. *Microfilm,* the record-keeping media of choice, will last several centuries before degrading. Computer-readable media, such as hard disk drives, require special care and handling and degrade within a decade. CDs and DVDs will last around 50 years. As older technology becomes obsolete, even retrieving records stored 10 years earlier becomes a labor-intensive and expensive task. It is not enough to keep the data from deteriorating. Even if the data remain perfectly intact in a word processing file on a disk, the data are useless if the word processor necessary to read the file is no longer installed on any computer or if the disk drive necessary to read the disk no longer exists. As a result, ensuring that all of the data in a digital archive remains accessible requires ensuring not only the integrity of the data but also maintaining the computer hardware and software necessary to access that data.

Privacy concerns also abound. Since 9/11, there have been several controversies related to putting information online about power plants, sewage treatment plants, reservoirs, and other public service facilities, based on the argument that doing so would make it easier for terrorists to attack such facilities. The information, however, is already a matter of public record. Advocates of making such information available online argue that the public has a right to access this information and that this added layer of *security through obscurity (STO)* is entirely imagined.

CONTROLLING ACCESS TO ONLINE INFORMATION

According to Warren Buffet, "It takes twenty years to build a reputation and five minutes to ruin it. If you think about that, you'll do things differently." There are a few ways to protect a reputation online. First, one should limit the information included in account profiles. One's friends already know one's birthday, address, and phone number. Avoid including anything that can be used by a stranger for identity theft. Second, take advantage of the privacy settings by turning them up to their highest level. Remove the ability for the social networking site to share information with other Web sites or with people who are not friends. Third, avoid polls or apps, as these are often simply ploys to collect personal information. Be particularly mindful of sensitive questions that may be used to secure accounts, including but not limited to social security numbers, passwords, city of birth, and mother's maiden name.

There are several software products that seek to limit the amount of negative information about a user that filters out onto the Web. One product, Reputation Defender, promises to *Googlewash* (place positive reports and biographies at the top of the Google search listings) any personal or company identity. Electronic Frontier Foundation (EFF) technology director Stanton McCandlish recommends some browser options that can prevent the spread of personally identifying information, including curtailing cookies, using throwaway e-mail addresses, and using encryption whenever possible.

ONLINE DATA: MORE UP-TO-DATE AND OBSOLETE THAN EVER

Because there is so much personal information available online from so many different sources, it can be difficult to keep track of it all. As a result, certain information is bound to become out-of-date. As a very simple example, when a user moves, he or she will certainly fail to update the new address in the hundreds of Web sites, bank accounts, utility accounts, and social networks where the information is stored. The result is that much of the information about a user may actually be obsolete.

Yet because the information is available online in electronic form, it can give the appearance that somehow it is accurate. In other words, the mere fact that data are stored in digital form can make this data misleading. This is particularly true because accurate records may not always be kept of when a particular piece of information was last updated. Therefore, if current information about a user is mixed together with old information, it may not be possible

Employers and Social Networking Sites

Job seekers must be aware that many employers now screen job applicants via social networking sites. According to *ComputerWorld,* in 2008 one in five employers used social networking sites to screen potential applicants and one in three job candidates was rejected because of information gleaned from social media sites. More recently, the Society for Human Resources Management (SHRM) found that in 2011 more than half of human resources professionals used social networking sites to screen job candidates. The data suggests that the number of employers using information from the Internet is steadily increasing.

After being hired, keeping Facebook clean of disparaging remarks about work, bosses, or customers is important too. A personal message board for airing thoughts and grievances to the world can be a powerful soapbox. Before publishing anything on Twitter, Facebook, YouTube, or anywhere else, users should be aware that the information can be seen by friends, bosses, and colleagues just as if it were posted on a bulletin board.

for the person or company who is storing the information, or for anyone who accesses such information, to easily detect which information is current and which is not.

Keeping this information consistent is vital in some circumstances. If there are multiple copies of a user's résumé online, then it is vital that they all list the same job history, so that an employer who checks does not suspect the user of lying about his or her past.

EXAMPLES OF WAYS IN WHICH INFORMATION BECOMES AVAILABLE ONLINE

In the early days of the Internet, information about private individuals rarely became available online unless someone chose to upload such information directly onto a Web site. In contrast, today a wide variety of information about an individual can become available online as the indirect result of that person's online activity, as in the case where someone sends an e-mail to a mailing list, and the mailing list is automatically archived to a public Web site. Personal information about an individual can even become available online as a result of the individual's offline activity, such as buying a house, participating in a high school sporting event, or making a donation to an event hosted by a charity. The following section explores just a few of the ways in which personal information can become available online.

Making Online Purchases

In the days before computers, purchases were rarely, if ever, tracked. As technology progressed, it became possible, then feasible, then profitable to track user spending habits. As a result, nearly every retailer, from the local Wal-Mart to online shopping giant Amazon, keeps a record of the items customers purchase. When customers search, bid, buy, participate in contests, post on forums, or communicate with customer service, retailers such as Amazon track user information, including names, billing and shipping addresses, phone numbers, credit card numbers, e-mail addresses, content of reviews, personal description, photographs, social security numbers, and driver's license numbers. This information is often shared with affiliated businesses and third-party service providers.

Posting to Message Boards or Forums

Many users, especially those recognized as experts in their field, post under their own name on message boards or forums. Many message boards are mirrored or archived, and this content is kept on the Web long after a user deletes the post or even after the Web site becomes defunct. Many posts from the late '80s and early '90s are still available on the Web and, as storage costs continue to decrease, more and more information will become archived forever.

Involuntary Disclosure

In many cases, a user's information may be disclosed accidentally or intentionally without notifying or obtaining permission from the user. Sometimes, this information is fairly harmless, such as award recipient listings or wedding announcements. At times, even these listings include hometowns, parents' names, and ages. In other instances, hackers who breach large databases have posted user information, including cell phone numbers and Social Security numbers, online.

When communicating online, users must always question how secure the information is. Credit card or bank information may be intercepted if the Web site does not provide encryption protection. Plaintext communication, such as instant messaging, is vulnerable to snooping as well. In 2010, online poker network Cereus used a weak encryption method instead of the industry standard SSL to deliver information to client's screens. Hackers on an unprotected wireless network could receive user names, passwords, addresses, account balances, and hole cards of anyone else on the network. The exposure of the flaw coincided with the World Series of Poker, when tens of thousands of poker players shared hotel rooms in Las Vegas. This is a known risk of wireless networking, which is quickly becoming ubiquitous.

Creating a Web Site or Social Profile

Because Facebook and other online social networks are marketed as ways to communicate informally with friends, people tend to take fewer precautions with the amount and kinds of information they disclose on such networks. For example, a user's date and place of birth are common information volunteered on social networking sites, but these may be answers to security questions asked by a bank to recover passwords or verify identities. By placing them out in the open, an unwitting user is more likely to be a victim of identity theft.

(continues on page 68)

Robert Ellis Smith, Privacy Advocate

Robert Ellis Smith is an attorney and a leading expert on privacy in the United States. A graduate of Harvard College and Georgetown Law Center, he had been a reporter, newspaper editor, and assistant director of civil rights at the U.S. Department of Health and Human Services. Smith is the publisher of the *Privacy Journal,* the oldest publication on the individual's right to privacy, which he founded in 1974. In fact, there was no field of privacy when the *Privacy Journal* was first published. The monthly newsletter provides updates on new technology and its impact on privacy and tips on how you can protect yourself and informs the reader on the most recent legal and legislative developments and corporate practices. In addition, Smith also publishes special reports and directories of privacy laws and experts, which attract just about as much interest from the subscribers as the *Journal* itself.

Smith, who was a newspaper reporter for nine years before enrolling at Georgetown University Law Center, never intended to practice law. However, his degree was useful in boosting his credentials with potential critics—nobody could accuse him of not being able to understand the legal underpinnings of a privacy argument. Smith became a known critic of the information collection practices as early as the 1970s, arguing that the information collected from individuals and stored on the computer, which was just becoming popular, was unnecessary, not always accurate, and difficult to verify. Because this information was being used for a variety of purposes, including access to credit and employment, Smith believed that it was important that credit report information be verifiably accurate and kept in a secure manner. He urged people not to provide unnecessary or unasked-for information to anyone who does not have a legitimate need to know it. Smith has also lobbied for a federal ban on the use of polygraph testing during preemployment security screening.

Although his concerns about the accuracy of credit reports did not attract a following in the 1980s when he first began to voice his concerns, over the next 10 years Smith became a thorn in the side of credit reporting companies. Smith believes that the involvement of consumer lobbyist groups influenced the way credit bureaus keep individuals' information, while the credit companies had always said that their procedures are more than adequate and benefit the consumer by providing him with more extensive choices stemming from knowing his likes and dislikes. Smith's biggest concern is that this sensitive information may be used to prepare credit scores and responses to employment background checks, potentially disseminating erroneous information that has not been verified by the consumer.

Even more important than safeguarding pieces of information such as Social Security numbers, bank account numbers, or credit card statements, Smith expressed doubt that Social Security numbers should be used at all due to their vulnerability to hackers. The first five digits of the Social Security number are easy to guess based on the time and location of the person's birth; the last four are harder to decipher. Therefore, it is

Robert Ellis Smith, privacy expert, advocate, and publisher of the *Privacy Journal (Kevin Kurdash, from www. privacyjournal.net)*

very important to keep less traditionally protected information about yourself, such as your date of birth and birth city, off the Internet, Facebook, or other social networking media sites, and limit the amount of information known about one's self in general.

Smith has taught at Harvard, Brown University, Emerson College, and the University of Maryland and was twice asked to write the definition of privacy for the *World Book Encyclopedia*. He uses his journalistic skills to stay abreast of all of the new developments in the realm of privacy, and his newsletter promises to keep the reader weeks ahead of the mainstream press or refund the cost of subscription. Smith frequently appears as an expert witness in privacy cases. He is the author of two books: *Privacy: How to Protect What's Left of It,* which was nominated for the National Book Award in 1980, and *Ben Franklin's Web Site: Privacy and Curiosity from Plymouth Rock to the Internet,* an acclaimed account of privacy throughout the history of the United States. Smith writes a regular column on privacy for *Forbes* magazine's Web site forbes.com.

(continued from page 65)

Using a pseudonym, or *screen name,* is a popular way of unlinking the online and real world. In some cases, however, users are encouraged or required to use their real name. Posting a résumé or creating a profile on Monster, Careerbuilder, or LinkedIn typically means providing a plethora of personally identifying information on a searchable database.

CONCLUSIONS

Until relatively recently in human history, there was a sharp distinction between private individuals and public figures. Until the 20th century, the latter category consisted of a tiny fraction of the world's population, including only royalty, politicians, religious leaders, and a small number of authors, painters, and other artists. With the rise of motion pictures, radio, and television, the ranks of celebrities grew to include a much larger number of athletes, actors, musicians, and other entertainers. Yet such public figures remained a relatively small percentage of the population.

A distinction has always been recognized between the standards of privacy that apply to public figures and those that apply to private individuals. The press considers itself justified in scrutinizing the professional activities and often the private lives of public figures in ways that would be considered improper if applied to the actions of private individuals. Elected officials, judges, and other public figures often are required to disclose private financial information to the public as part of the process of determining whether they are qualified to hold office. The law even recognizes that statements that would be considered slanderous (and therefore unlawful) if made about private individuals can be protected under the First Amendment when made about public figures, unless such statements are made with reckless disregard for the truth.

The Internet, however, is blurring the line between public and private figures. An individual blogger who writes from a laptop in his or her living room can achieve greater readership and notoriety than an anchorperson on a local broadcast television news station. Homemade videos created in minutes using a Web cam and posted to YouTube frequently become viral sensations, reaching millions of viewers around the world, often making their creators famous (at least for a short time). A local business owner who runs for sheriff in a small town and makes an inappropriate statement in a campaign speech to a crowd of a dozen people can find his comments spread like wildfire on Twitter just minutes later.

Such effects do not merely increase the number of people who qualify as public figures. At least two features of Internet celebrity differ from the past. First, the Internet makes it possible to transform someone from an unknown to a household name literally overnight. In the past, even so-called overnight successes typically spent years building their careers before finally becoming recognized by a national audience. Second, most celebrities in the past made some conscious effort to achieve their status. Today, many Internet sensations find themselves receiving international attention as the result of their actions being publicized by someone else (perhaps through a video taken on a cell phone) or because they did not think through the possible implications of posting what they considered to be a private video on YouTube.

Because yesterday's public figures had time to prepare themselves for their public status and make some conscious decision to expose themselves to public scrutiny, there was some justification for thinking that criticizing or even openly mocking celebrities would have limited impact on the celebrities themselves. They were expected to have developed a thick skin in the face of satire and to understand that their private lives would be at least partially public.

Today's Internet celebrities often enter the limelight unprepared to cross the dividing line between private and public life. For example, the so-called Star Wars kid was a high school student who made a video of himself clumsily swinging a golf ball retriever as if it were a light saber from the film *Star Wars*. One of his schoolmates discovered the tape. The tape was then passed from person to person and eventually posted on the Internet, where it quickly spread like wildfire. According to some estimates, the video, first posted in 2002, has now been viewed more than 900 million times. Most people who view and laugh at the video do not recognize the pain that it has caused the boy pictured in it, who never intended for the tape to become public. His parents eventually filed a lawsuit against some of the students responsible for posting the video to the Internet, claiming that their son would "be under psychiatric care for an indefinite amount of time" because of the harassment and ridicule he continued to face as a result of the posting of the video.

Whether or not such a lawsuit has merit, the claims underlying it are worth considering. Being transformed from a private to a public figure, particularly overnight and unintentionally, can be a trying experience even for businesspeople, teachers, community leaders, and others who have experience dealing with the public on a small scale. The Internet now makes it possible for anyone, of any age and background, to become a celebrity instantly and worldwide. At the very least, everyone can take responsibility for respecting the rights and feelings of others by thinking very carefully before hitting send on a message that has the potential to expose the private acts of others to a public audience.

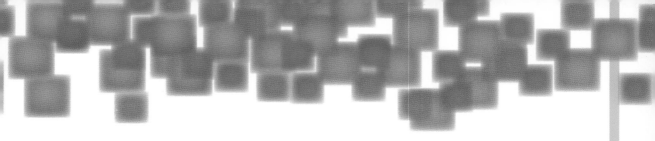

6

IDENTITY THEFT: PROTECTING ONESELF AGAINST IMPOSTERS

Identity theft is the misuse of *personally identifying information*—one's name, Social Security number, credit card numbers, or other personal and financial information. To a thief, this information is an open door to bank accounts, charge cards, and easy money. Victims of this crime may not find out about the theft until their credit reports or credit card statements arrive bearing charges they never made—or, worse, when they are contacted by debt collectors.

Skilled identity thieves may use a variety of methods to get hold of this information, such as:

- Rummaging through trash in search of bank statements or bills.
- Skimming credit or debit card numbers during transactions at stores or restaurants.
- Diverting the victim's billing statements to another location by completing a fraudulent change of address form.
- Stealing wallets, mail, preapproved credit offers, new checks, or tax information. A dishonest employee may steal personnel or financial records from a business.
- Phishing, an online practice in which thieves impersonate financial institutions or companies and send spam or pop-up messages to entice victims to reveal personal information.
- Hacking into large companies' Web sites or databases and snatching customers' personal information.

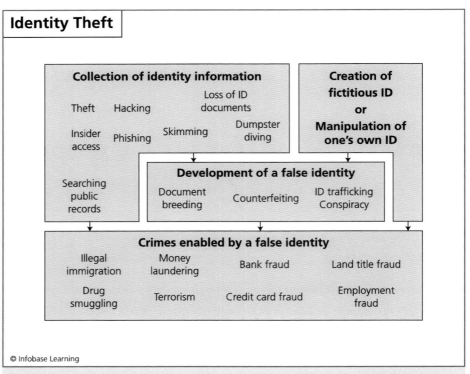

False identities may be developed in a variety of ways. For example, one can start by modifying one's own real identification (ID), by creating a false ID from scratch, or by collecting information about someone else's identity, such as by searching public records or using a phishing scheme to obtain someone else's Social Security number. Such initial steps may provide the foundation for the development of a false identity, which may in turn facilitate the commission of crimes such as money laundering, bank fraud, and even terrorism.

Once they have the personal information, identity thieves can open new credit card accounts in the victims' names, open new phone or wireless accounts on someone else's dime, or run up charges on existing accounts. They may create counterfeit checks, open a bank account in the victim's name and write bad checks, or even take out a loan under an assumed name. Some victims even discover their personal information has been given to police during an arrest.

The Federal Trade Commission (FTC) estimates that as many as 9 million Americans have their identities stolen each year. Identity theft and related fraud were up considerably in 2009, with 11.2 million victims at an estimated cost of $54 billion dollars. In 2008, just less than 10 million people were victims, at an estimated cost of $48 billion. Identity theft is serious. While some victims can resolve their problems quickly, others spend hundreds of dollars and many hours repairing damage to their bank accounts and reputations. Identity theft may cause people to lose out on job opportunities or be denied loans because of negative information on their credit reports.

PROTECTING ONE'S IDENTITY

The first evidence of identity theft often shows up in bank accounts and credit statements. Wise consumers check bank statements carefully each month and also check their credit reports on a regular basis. Unfortunately, many people learn that their identity has been compromised only after some damage has already been done. Bill collection agencies may contact them for overdue debts they never incurred or they may apply for a mortgage or car loan and learn that problems with their credit history are holding up the loan. They may be tipped off by mail about an apartment they never rented, a house they never bought, or a job they never held.

The FTC advises a person who believes his or her identity has been stolen to take the following steps as quickly as possible and keep a record with the details of conversations and copies of all correspondence.

1. **Review credit reports and place a fraud alert.** Contact the toll-free fraud number of any of the three major consumer reporting companies (listed below) to request a fraud alert. One call will be sufficient; each company is required to contact the other two, which will also place alerts on the victim's reports.

   - **TransUnion:** 1-800-680-7289; www.transunion.com; Fraud Victim Assistance Division, P.O. Box 6790, Fullerton, CA 92834-6790
   - **Equifax:** 1-800-525-6285; www.equifax.com; P.O. Box 740241, Atlanta, GA 30374-0241
   - **Experian:** 1-888-EXPERIAN (397-3742); www.experian.com; P.O. Box 9554, Allen, TX 75013

   Once the fraud alert is on file, the customer is entitled to a free copy of his or her credit report from each consumer reporting company. Check these carefully for inquiries from strange companies, accounts the consumer did not open, and unexplained debts. Verify personal information, such as Social Security number, address, name or initials, and employer. Continue to check credit reports periodically, especially for the first year after the identity theft is discovered, to make sure no new fraudulent activity has occurred.

2. **Close accounts that have been tampered with or opened fraudulently.** Call and speak with someone in the security or fraud department of each company that appears in a suspicious entry on the credit report. Follow up in writing and include copies (not originals) of supporting documents. Notify credit card companies and banks in writing. Send letters by certified mail and request return receipts to help document what the company received and when. Keep a file of correspondence and enclosures. When opening new accounts, use all-new personal identification numbers (PINs) and passwords. Avoid using easily available information to answer security questions. Once the identity theft dispute has been resolved, ask for written statements confirming that compromised accounts have been closed and fraudulent debts have been discharged.

3. **File a complaint with the FTC.** Use the FTC's online complaint form or call the Identity Theft Hotline, toll-free: 1-877-ID-THEFT (438-4338); TTY: 1-866-653-4261; or write Identity Theft Clearinghouse, Federal Trade Commission, 600 Pennsylvania Avenue NW, Washington, DC 20580. Filing a report with the FTC provides important information that can help law enforcement officials across the nation track down and stop identity thieves. The FTC can refer victims' complaints to other government agencies and companies for further action, as well as investigate companies for violations of laws the agency enforces.

4. **File a report with the police.** If the police are reluctant to take a report, ask to file a miscellaneous incident report or try another jurisdiction, such as the state police. Another option is to check with the state attorney general's office to find out if state law requires the police to take reports for identity theft. A list of state attorneys general is available online at www.naag.org.

It is difficult to predict how long the effects of identity theft may linger. Many factors play a role, including the type of theft, whether the thief sold or passed the information on to other thieves, whether the thief is caught, and problems related to correcting the victim's credit report. Victims of identity theft should monitor financial records for several months after they discover the crime. Victims should review their credit reports once every three months in the first year of the theft, and once a year thereafter. Stay alert for other signs of identity theft.

MALWARE, SOCIAL ENGINEERING, AND IDENTITY THEFT

Computers often serve as useful tools to those engaging in identity theft. Malware, short for malicious software, is designed to secretly access a computer system without the owner's permission. The term applies to a variety of forms of hostile, intrusive, or annoying software. Data-stealing malware can work in several ways, such as waiting for the user to access banking Web sites, then imitating the sites' pages to steal customers' sensitive information; or covertly monitoring victims' Web-surfing habits, then uploading data to a server that produces targeted pop-up ads. Other types of spyware steal personal information, such as account names and passwords, related to online games.

Online phishing is a type of social engineering that tricks computer users into revealing personal or financial information through a fraudulent e-mail message or Web site. A common online phishing scam starts with an e-mail message that looks like an official notice from a trusted source, such as a bank, credit card company, or reputable online merchant. In the e-mail message, recipients are directed to a fraudulent Web site where they are asked to provide personal information, such as an account number or password. This information is then usually used for identity theft.

Governments and corporations have instituted a number of laws and safeguards to try to prevent identity theft. Consumers are increasingly asked to answer multiple security questions and enter longer and more complex—thus harder to copy—passwords. The Department of Justice prosecutes cases of identity theft and fraud under a variety of federal statutes. In 1998, for example, Congress passed the Identity Theft and Assumption Deterrence Act. This legislation created a new offense of identity theft, which prohibits "knowingly transferring or using, without lawful authority, a means of identification of another person with the intent to commit, or to aid or abet, any unlawful activity that constitutes a violation of Federal law, or that constitutes a felony under any applicable State or local law."

PROMINENT EXAMPLES OF IDENTITY THEFT

Several large-scale identity thefts have made the news in recent years:

- In April 2005, the company that owns the LexisNexis legal and business information service reported that more than 310,000 people's accounts had been breached. The compromised information included names, addresses, Social Security, and driver licenses' numbers. LexisNexis notified the individuals and offered them free support services, including credit bureau reports, credit monitoring for one year, and fraud insurance.
- In May 2006, a longtime analyst at the U.S. Department of Veterans Affairs (VA) was blamed for the theft of 26.5 million veterans' Social Security numbers after he took sensitive data home and his home was burglarized, the agency said. The stolen data included names, Social Security numbers, dates of birth, and disability ratings. The government organization sent many thousands of letters to veterans and their spouses with the bad news that they were at heightened risk for identity theft.
- In March 2010, a 28-year-old Miami man was sentenced to 20 years in prison in connection with the largest identity theft case in U.S. history. Albert Gonzalez admitted to leading an international ring that stole 40 million credit and debit card records from U.S. retailers including Target, TJ Maxx, Office Max, and BJ's Wholesale Club. He took advantage of vulnerabilities in computer security systems to access customers' card numbers.
- In April 2011, Hackers got into Sony's PlayStation Network and Qriocity online music and film service by exploiting a known security vulnerability, giving the intruders access to personal customer data from Sony Online Entertainment, including 23,400 credit and debit card records and personal account information of 24.6 million account holders (such as the account holder's name, birthdate, and mother's maiden name). Sony claims that customers' credit card numbers were encrypted and therefore would be difficult for hackers

The Children's Online Privacy Protection Act (COPPA)

Whether studying, shopping, surfing, or chatting, kids take advantage of everything the Internet has to offer. But when it comes to their personal information, the FTC puts their parents in the drivers' seats.

Under the Children's Online Privacy Protection Act (COPPA) and regulations enforced by the FTC, anyone who operates a Web site directed at children under 13—or a general Web site that might appeal to kids—must comply with COPPA's two main requirements when collecting personal information. First, information security practices must be posted prominently on the home page and wherever users are asked for information. These include what information is collected; how it is collected; how the information is used; whether it is given to third parties; and how parents can control the information. Second, before the companies collect, use, or disclose a child's information, COPPA requires them to notify parents and obtain their consent.

COPPA was first implemented in April 2000, following a three-year effort by the FTC to identify and educate industry and the public about the issues raised by the online collection of personal information from children and adult consumers. A March 1998 survey of 212 commercial children's Web sites found that while 89 percent of the sites collected personal information from children, only 24 percent posted privacy policies and only 1 percent required parental consent to the collection or disclosure of children's information. The act received widespread support from industry and consumer groups.

The FTC's December 2008 settlement with Sony BMG Music Entertainment shows the importance of COPPA compliance. Sony Music operates Web sites dedicated to their entertainers, including numerous artists popular with children and teenagers. Many of these sites allow users to create personal fan pages, post reviews, upload photos or videos, and post comments in online forums. To register, Sony Music required users to submit a broad range of personal information, including their date of birth. According to the FTC, Sony Music knowingly collected personal information from at least 30,000 underage children without first getting their parents' consent. As a result, children were able to interact with Sony Music fans of all ages, including adults. The FTC filed a complaint against Sony, which eventually led to a $1 million civil penalty against the entertainment company for COPPA violations.

to decipher. In response to the security breach, Sony offered users of the PlayStation Network the option to sign up for free identity theft protection for one year.

Such breaches continue to occur despite the best efforts of some of the world's leading technology companies. The continued ability of identity thieves to exploit security vulnerabilities and gain access to sensitive personal information should act as a warning to all computer users to take every possible step to minimize the likelihood that their identities will be stolen and to act promptly to take advantage of any post-theft assistance offered by government agencies and companies to individuals whose personal information has been compromised.

NOT ALL WEB SITES ARE CREATED EQUAL

Identity thieves can be crafty, and the online world can seem complex and full of dangers. But consumers can rely on common sense and a variety of other safeguards for protection against identity theft.

Web sites with any of the following features might not be trustworthy:

- A large number of pop-up advertisements or windows.
- Offers of downloads or products that seem too good to be true, such as expensive software for free or a very low price.
- Frequent misspellings or bad grammar.
- Games or quizzes that require personal information before completing the game or revealing quiz answers.
- Objectionable content, such as pornography or illegal materials.
- Request for a credit card number or other personal information as verification of identity that seems unnecessary.
- A lack of security certifications for purchases or other credit card transactions.

Software is available that alerts users to Web sites that are known or suspected to contain malware or other identity theft risks. Two common free tools are Netcraft Toolbar and McAfee SiteAdvisor, available for Internet Explorer and Firefox. Web browsers also offer tools to help control and protect users' information. Most browsers show an alert when a Web site uses SSL, a security measure that encrypts personal data. The browser may indicate this by displaying a padlock icon (typically in the browser's toolbar) or by highlighting the Web site's name in the address bar in green. A user can click on the padlock icon or the green-highlighted name to view more information about the site's encryption and certification. Users of popular browsers, such as Firefox, Explorer, or Safari, should update them frequently to take full advantage of the most recent privacy features.

Trustworthy Web sites have signs to watch for:

- The site is owned by a well-known company or organization. However, even if the company seems trustworthy, always read the privacy or terms of use statement.
- The site's address begins with HTTPS rather than HTTP.
- The site features seals of approval from an Internet trust organization (such as TRUSTe), which verifies that a Web site has a privacy statement and gives consumers a choice of how their information is used. However, these seals are no automatic guarantee; if a user has reason to suspect a trust logo is questionable, he or she should contact the trust organization for confirmation.
- The site requests credit card numbers or similar information only if there is a good reason to do so. The entry form for recording information is secure.
- Reliable friends, colleagues, or publications vouch for the site.

PASSWORD CREATION AND MANAGEMENT

Cyber criminals have sophisticated tools to guess passwords associated with users' accounts. Some passwords are easier to guess than others. Therefore, to avoid becoming the victim of identity theft, it is critical to use strong passwords on all online accounts.

The keys to password strength are length and complexity. Many Web sites have specific requirements for passwords, but an ideal password will commonly be at least eight characters long and contain letters, punctuation, symbols, and numbers. Security experts recommend the following safeguards when selecting a password:

- Whenever possible, use at least 14 characters.
- Include a wide variety of characters; the wider, the better.

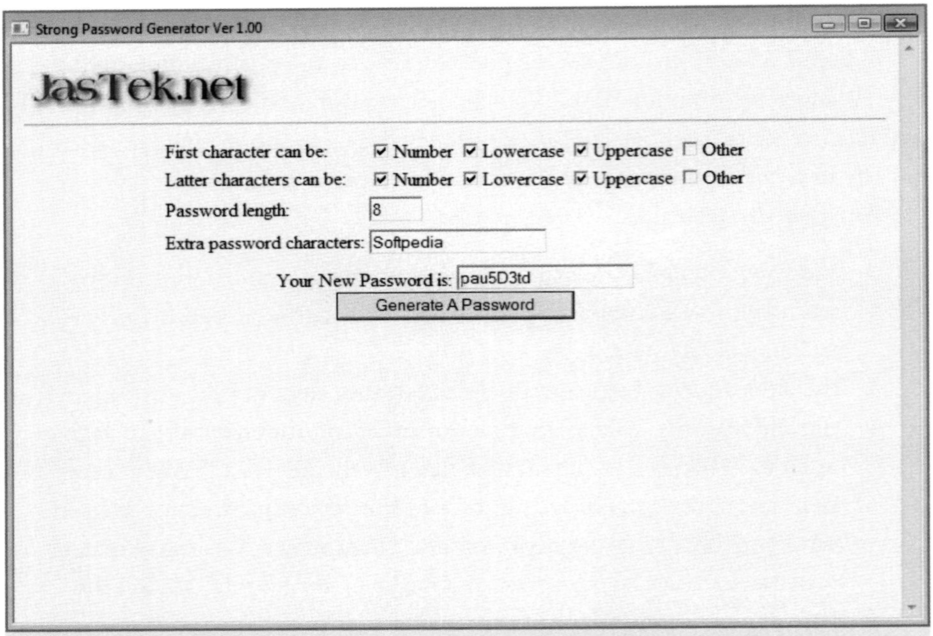

Passwords that are strong, and therefore hard for others to guess, are difficult to create. Fortunately, various software packages exist for automatically generating and securely storing strong passwords. This screenshot shows one such software package, which has generated a strong password automatically. Once such a password is generated, it may be copied and pasted into a Web browser or other software without having to retype it manually. Such software is much more reliable than humans at creating strong, random passwords. *(Strong Password Generator by James A. Smith)*

- Use the entire keyboard, not just the letters and characters used most often.
- Choose something that is easy to remember, but do not connect it to personal information, such as a pet's name or the user's birthday.
- Avoid using words that can be found in a dictionary. That includes words spelled backward, common misspellings, and abbreviations.
- Avoid sequences or repeated characters, such as 12345678, 222222, abcdefg, or adjacent letters on the keyboard (qwerty).
- Use different passwords for different Web sites and services.

The easiest way to remember passwords is to write them down—but put them in a secure spot, not in a computer file or on a scrap of paper stuck to the

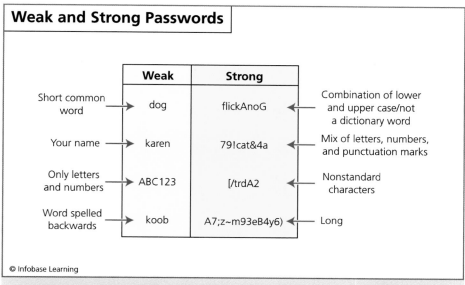

Weak and Strong Passwords

	Weak	Strong	
Short common word	dog	flickAnoG	Combination of lower and upper case/not a dictionary word
Your name	karen	79!cat&4a	Mix of letters, numbers, and punctuation marks
Only letters and numbers	ABC123	[/trdA2	Nonstandard characters
Word spelled backwards	koob	A7;z~m93eB4y6)	Long

© Infobase Learning

Although many people use their names, telephone numbers, dates of birth, and addresses as passwords, such passwords are very weak because they are easy for others to guess quickly. Examples of weak passwords are common words (particularly if they contain only a few letters), people's names, combinations of letters and numbers but not other kinds of characters, and common words spelled backward. Examples of strong passwords are those that contain a combination of at least 10 lowercase and uppercase characters, a mix of alphanumeric characters and punctuation marks, and nonstandard characters (such as /, &, and @).

monitor. Do not share them with friends, family members, or coworkers. Never provide a password via e-mail or in response to an e-mail request. Avoid typing passwords on public computers, such as those in Internet cafes, computer labs, or libraries. Cyber criminals can purchase keystroke-logging devices that gather information typed on public computers, including passwords. Some e-mail providers will give users single-use codes. Upon request, a single-use authentication code is delivered to the user's mobile phone. The code, instead of a password, can be used to access e-mail on a public machine.

Users with a long list of complex passwords to remember may wish to use password management software, which uses a master password to keep personal information secure. When the user visits a Web site, the software enters the secret, encrypted, strong password for the account. Some widely used

(continues on page 84)

Marc Rotenberg, Privacy Advocate

Mark Rotenberg is an attorney and executive director of the Electronic Privacy Information Center (EPIC), a public interest research group in Washington, D.C., established in 1994 to protect privacy and constitutional and civil liberties in the age of technological and information advancement. Born in 1961 in Boston, Rotenberg is a son of a Boston realtor. His parents were active in social causes; he remembers marching in Vietnam War protests with his brother and parents as a child. He is no stranger to technology and computers: As an undergraduate student at Harvard, he taught computer science courses to freshmen. Today, Rotenberg is a leading online privacy activist and an expert on Internet law and policy. A graduate of Harvard College and Stanford Law School, he served as counsel to Senator Patrick J. Leahy on the Senate Judiciary Committee. Mr. Rotenberg teaches information privacy law at Georgetown Law Center. He has

Marc Rotenberg, privacy expert and executive director of the Electronic Privacy Information Center (EPIC), shown here speaking at the U.S. Senate commerce hearing on computer spam in 2003 *(Scott J. Ferrell/*Congressional Quarterly/*Alamy)*

provided testimony before Congress on issues such as access to information, consumer protection, computer security, and communications privacy. Mr. Rotenberg has served on numerous international advisory panels and chairs the American Bar Association's Committee on Privacy and Information Protection. He is the former chairman of the Public Interest Registry, which manages the ".org" domain. He is the editor of *Privacy and Human Rights* and *The Privacy Law Sourcebook* and coeditor of *Information Privacy Law.*

Rotenberg has been outspoken about the need for transparency among companies that collect personal data from consumers, such as social networking Web sites, search engines, and stores that issue club cards to frequent shoppers, with respect to how the information is used and stored. These organizations collect a variety of information about individuals and aspects of their private lives and, as a rule, do not disclose the kind of analysis that they perform on this data or what happens to it after it is collected. For example, a search engine like Google tracks individual's searches and is able to tailor advertisements to an individual person's interests based on the searches they complete. However, Google is not subject to privacy laws, such as the Health Insurance Portability and Accountability Act (HIPAA), which would prohibit it from releasing information about someone doing online research on a particular illness or medication to an insurance company. The insurance company may use that information in their coverage determination for that individual. In Rotenberg's opinion, one's ability to know when and what data is collected, as well as the ability to control dissemination of personal information, are key elements of privacy. One must also be able to make sure that information is being requested for the right reasons and that there is a legitimate need for collecting it. The lack of regulation and the absence of strict rules regarding how personal information must be handled by these organizations both presents an opportunity for identity theft and subjects individuals to unnecessary observation by third parties.

Rotenberg is also opposed to the REAL ID, the proposed national identity card, which was approved by Congress in 2005. While the card's ease of use would simplify the process of retrieving data from it, this very process is potentially troubling for the privacy of the individual. The card's ability to be scanned by anyone in possession of a reader may allow unauthorized access to the information it contains. Because the card is to be read remotely, one has no clear indication of when the information is being collected, and one may not even fully know what information is being gathered from one's own card at any point in time. In addition, the collection process itself exposes very sensitive personal information to an opportunity to be intercepted by an unauthorized third party during the transmission.

In addition to his work in the area of privacy law, Rotenberg is a tournament chess player and won the 2007 Washington, D.C., Chess Championship.

(continued from page 81)
software includes LastPass, RoboForm, and Norton IdentitySafe. Of course, a compromised master password renders all of the protected passwords vulnerable. A single password may be more convenient, but it also carries more risk.

Users seeking simple online storage of passwords may find the online password manager Password++ useful. The free application requires credentials for access to the site. The advantages of online password managers over desktop-based versions are portability and a reduced risk of losing passwords through theft from or damage to a single computer. The major disadvantage, however, is that the user must trust the hosting site's security practices.

CONCLUSIONS

Identity theft is easier to commit in the age of the Internet for at least two reasons. First, private information about individuals is available in greater quantity and more widely than ever before. Second, the lack of face-to-face contact in online interactions makes it easier for an identity thief to convincingly impersonate others online. Although Internet users can take some personal responsibility for protecting themselves against identity theft, such as by visiting only trusted Web sites and using responsible password-management practices, personal responsibility is not sufficient to protect against all identity theft. Inside jobs by employees of government agencies and corporations and hacking, as in incidents in 2011 at Sony, Fox News, PBS, to name but a few, can succeed at stealing the identities of thousands of people at a time, even when those people have taken all possible steps to protect themselves.

Online identity theft will likely never disappear entirely because it results from an inherent feature of using computers and the Internet to communicate—the use of limited pieces of electronic data, such as user names, passwords, and Social Security numbers, as proxies (substitutes) for direct personal knowledge of a person's identity. Just as the U.S. Treasury continually adds new features to paper currency in an attempt to overcome the latest efforts at counterfeiting, so too will continuous vigilance be necessary to keep the incidence of identity theft at a minimum.

7

KEEPING YOUR DATA SECURE: THE BEST OFFENSE IS A GOOD DEFENSE

Viruses, spyware, phishing artists, and identity thieves can only truly succeed if they can access and understand the information they copy, just as stealing a message written in French is of no value to a thief who only reads English. This chapter explores some of the ways in which individual computer users can take matters into their own hands by using encryption and other technologies to protect their computers, software, and data against theft and damage.

WHAT IS ENCRYPTION?

Encryption is the conversion of data into a form that cannot be easily understood by unauthorized users. *Decryption* is the process of returning encrypted data to its original form, so it can be understood. The use of encryption is as old as the art of communication—think of wartime *ciphers* used to keep the enemy from obtaining the contents of transmissions. (Ciphers are often incorrectly called codes. Technically, a code is a means of representing a signal without the intent of keeping it secret, such as Morse code.) Simple ciphers include the substitution of letters for numbers or the rotation of letters in the alphabet. More sophisticated ciphers use complex computer algorithms to encode plain text into nonreadable form to ensure privacy. The recipient of the encrypted text uses a key to decode the message, returning it to its original plain text form.

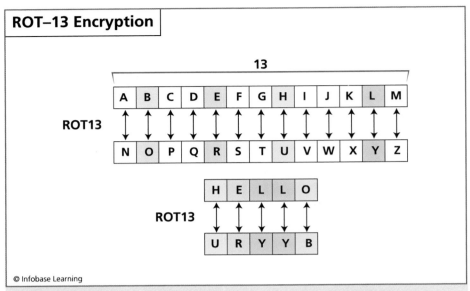

ROT–13 Encryption

© Infobase Learning

One of the simplest kinds of encryption is ROT-13 encryption, which encrypts a message by rotating the characters in the message by 13 letters. In other words, each letter from A–M is replaced by the letter that appears 13 positions later in the alphabet and each letter from N–Z is replaced by the letter that appears 13 positions earlier in the alphabet. The reverse replacements are applied to the encrypted message to decrypt it. Although messages that have been encrypted using ROT-13 are difficult for humans to read by sight, they are not suitable for carrying sensitive information because they can be decrypted nearly instantly by computer software.

Until the advent of the Internet, encryption was primarily a military tool, rarely used by the general public. Today, with online marketing, banking, health care, etc., all computer users should be aware of how encryption can protect their personal information. Though most Internet browsers automatically encrypt information when connected to a secure Web site, many people choose to encrypt e-mail correspondence as well. Popular e-mail clients, such as Microsoft Office and Hotmail, feature easy-to-use security *plug-ins.* The most long-standing encryption standard is called *Pretty Good Privacy (PGP),* a humble name for a very strong military-grade encryption tool. PGP allows one to not only encrypt e-mail messages, but also personal files and folders.

Encryption can be used to protect data "at rest," such as computer files and folders stored on internal or external hard drives or removable *Universal Serial Bus (USB) flash drives.* In recent years, there have been numerous reports of con-

Public Key Encryption

Many types of encryption are available, but not all of them are reliable. The same computer that provides strong encryption can be used to break weak encryption schemes. Initially, 64-bit encryption was thought to be quite strong, but today 128-bit encryption is the standard, and this will undoubtedly change again in the future. Encryption schemes are categorized as symmetric or asymmetric. Symmetric key algorithms have a single, prearranged key that is shared between sender and receiver. This key both encrypts and decrypts text. Asymmetric encryption provides an extra level of security by creating a key pair for the user: a public key and a private key. The public key can be published online, and any sender can use it to transmit encrypted text. Once encrypted, the text can be decrypted only by the private key's owner using the owner's private key. Since its development in the middle 1970s, *public key encryption* (also known as asymmetric key encryption) has become the underpinning of many Internet security standards.

To implement public key encryption on a large scale, such as for a secure Web server, a different approach is required. This is where *digital certificates* come in. A digital certificate is basically a unique piece of code or a large number that says that the Web server is trusted by an independent source known as a certificate authority. The certificate authority acts as a middleman that both computers trust. It confirms that each computer is in fact who it says it is and then provides the public keys of each computer to the other.

fidential data being exposed through loss or theft of laptops or backup drives. Encrypting such files helps protect them when other physical security measures fail. Encryption is also used to protect data in transit, such as data being transferred via networks, such as the Internet, mobile phones, wireless connections, Bluetooth devices, and automatic teller machines.

ENCRYPTING DATA ON COMPUTERS AND ONLINE

When any file is transferred from the Web server to a local disk, it must go across the Internet, through wires, and sometimes through the air. The data often travels in unencrypted form. A hacker with sufficient knowledge, technology, and access to a compromised system can intercept these transmissions. Depending on the type of data being transmitted, this may or may not be a concern. Sensitive data can be any information that, if stolen, could potentially result in damage to a private computer user, business, or organization. Examples include Social Security numbers, credit card numbers, student grades, financial aid data, and individuals' health information. Most people's computers contain information that they would prefer not to share with the general public. The use of secure encryption allows users to protect personal messages and important business correspondence at every point along its path.

A number of encryption tools, both commercial and open source, are available to computer users. Some are already part of operating systems, such as Windows, or included with Internet service providers' packages. Many of them are based on the PGP standard. Several examples include:

- GNU Privacy Guard—a free implementation of the OpenPGP standard. Supports a dozen encryption schemes, paired keys, and expiring signatures. Can be used on a variety of operating systems, such as Microsoft, Linux, or Mac OS.
- Disk Utility—a diverse tool that can create secure disk images and file volumes encrypted with AES 128-bit or 256-bit encryption. Available only for Macs.
- TrueCrypt—can create secure encrypted virtual disks or encrypt entire drives. Files are decrypted as they are accessed and modified, then encrypted when not in use.

Products such as PGP Desktop can be used to encrypt the entire hard drive, but users may have only a few files requiring that level of protection. Many commonly used software programs, such as Quicken, Google Docs, and most Microsoft Office applications, contain encryption tools that can be used to protect individual files.

Encrypting an e-mail message in Microsoft Office Outlook 2010 protects the privacy of the message by converting it from readable plaintext into scrambled cyphertext. Only the recipient who has the private key can unlock the coded messages. If an encrypted message is sent to a recipient whose e-mail setup does not support encryption, Outlook notifies the sender and offers the option of sending the message in unencrypted format. This process also encrypts any attachments sent with encrypted messages. Mozilla Firefox also offers encryption tools for its e-mail application.

Google Docs offers encryption, as long as users use https://docs.google.com instead of http://docs.google.com. The extra "s" means "secure." The only downside is that the secure site is a little slower. Setting encryption on a Quicken transaction or account attachment is simple: Just click on the blue underlined "encrypt" to turn encryption on or off for an attachment. A message at the top of the screen for viewing the attachment will alert the user that the attachment cannot be viewed outside of Quicken, with the option to unscramble the image. Note that encrypting attachments in Quicken make the images unreadable only outside of an individual's personal software. For true data security, the user should also use a file password.

Another option for sending private data is a Web-based e-mail encryption service. These tools do the work of encrypting the data; the sender just needs to create a password and click send. The recipient visits the service's site and enters the password to decrypt the e-mail.

There are several ways to ensure that files, data, or information are being transmitted in encrypted form. The user should make sure Web applications are transmitting over HTTPS instead of HTTP. Most browsers indicate security by displaying an icon that looks like a lock. The owner of a Web site who wants to transmit over HTTPS can purchase an SSL security certificate. When downloading files, consumers should use secured FTP rather than regular FTP. HTTPS protocol may be unavailable for some sites. Users should make sure the passwords they create for those accounts are strong, using at least eight characters and including letters, punctuation, symbols, and numbers. The passwords should also be different than those used for banking sites or other accounts containing sensitive information. That way, even if the former password is compromised, the more critical one is not.

BACKUP SECURITY

Most computer users understand the importance of periodically backing up files. Many of them probably learned the lesson the hard way, when a system crashed, taking with it critical information or hours of work. However, backup and security—both critical processes—can have opposing goals. Security procedures require tight control over who can access a user's data. Backup software, on the other hand, is optimized to simplify access, sometimes to a different platform or different location and often by someone other than the original owner of the data.

All the effort involved in encrypting data and communications can be wasted if a user backs up that data in unencrypted form. This can be a major security loophole, even in large corporations. The improper handling of data backups—which essentially represent all of an organization's assets—can lead to breaches of privacy, confidentiality, and regulatory compliance. Aside from public embarrassment, such losses and unauthorized disclosure can expose corporate assets and, more important, private client records.

There are several common tools for backing up computer data: CD/DVD-ROMs, external hard drives, flash drives, USB drives, and remote storage via the Internet. Securing backups involves not only encryption, but also ensuring the physical security of backup media, which can be subject to theft, loss, and damage. Online services help protect against hard drive failures and file corruption on an individual computer and can be less labor intensive than burning backup discs or manually backing up to an external hard drive. Most storage services use at least 128-bit encryption to transfer files and another form of encryption to protect data residing on servers. Some services also allow users to choose a private encryption key. This encrypts data on the user's machine rather than on the company's servers, thus providing a higher level of security during transfers. However, if the user loses or forgets that encryption key, the backup service cannot supply it. Experts warn that online backup is not a replacement for backups on an external hard drive, but keeping a remote backup can be good secondary protection. Many online backup services, such as CrashPlan and Mozy, offer online and local backups for a single price.

The problem of security is complicated by the fact that a great deal of data these days is stored in the cloud, where shared remote servers provide resources, software, and data to computers and other devices on demand. For example, a cloud-based word processor, such as Google Docs, stores documents on Google's servers rather than on the hard drive of the user's personal computer, even though from the user's perspective it may appear as if the document is stored on the user's computer. As a result, data in a Google Docs account, and in many other cloud-based accounts, such as accounts on Facebook and Amazon, is not under the user's direct control. This can make it difficult for the user to control security and backups of such data. The Cloud Security Alliance is a non-profit organization that addresses these developing issues, provides education, and promotes the use of best practices for providing security assurance within cloud computing.

WIRELESS SECURITY

Wireless networking has grown rapidly in popularity as a result of the convenience it offers. Wireless laptops, handheld computers, e-readers, smart phones, and iPads are everywhere today. Transmitting network communications through the air, however, makes such communications much more susceptible to interception. Even within a single building, a wireless signal can be intercepted by unauthorized users. More dangerous still, wireless signals typically cannot be contained within a building and are susceptible to interference from outside. (See the section "War-driving" below.) Because Wi-Fi access typically defaults to an encryption-free, or open, mode, users must take special steps to ensure wireless security.

One of the earliest wireless encryption standards, *Wired Equivalent Privacy* (WEP), proved vulnerable to hackers. The latest encryption technology, *Wi-Fi Protected Access (WPA2),* was introduced in 2004 and has been required in Wi-Fi certified products since April 2006. It supports Advanced Encryption Standard (AES), the most advanced encryption standard, which is also endorsed by the U.S. government. The *Wi-Fi Alliance* recommends that users select equipment supporting WPA2 to help protect their network from attacks to their security and privacy. In addition to using the latest encryption technology, computer users should take the following steps to ensure wireless security of their own networks and computers:

- Turn on encryption.
- Configure Wi-Fi devices to enable security protections.
- Utilize user names and passwords on devices, and change the password regularly. Select a high-quality password with at least eight characters and a mixture of upper- and lowercase letters and symbols. A strong password should not include personal information, such as name, birthdate, or address.

Wardriving

Wardriving refers to picking up wireless signals from a building simply by driving near it. Wireless network signals can travel for several hundred feet, making them accessible from adjacent buildings, streets, or parking lots. This gained attention in the early days of wireless networks, when many individuals, companies, and government agencies established wireless networks but did not secure them. Wardrivers, using a laptop, freely available software, a standard Wi-Fi card, and a GPS device, could log the status and location of wireless networks. They would then mark the location of open networks on the side of a building with chalked graffiti or publish the location on the Internet.

The term originated with the 1983 film *WarGames,* in which a young Matthew Broderick portrayed a character who used a computer to dial many phone numbers in hopes of finding an active modem. Broderick's character hacks into a government computer system to play a game and inadvertently puts the country at risk of nuclear attack.

Many early practitioners of wardriving acted more out of mischief than malice. The annual Las Vegas hackers' conference known as DEF CON started in 2002 with a competitive wardriving event. Two dozen teams drove through the streets of the city on a Saturday afternoon, scoring points for each unprotected wireless network they could locate and tap. Even the Massachusetts Institute of

- Configure Wi-Fi devices for approved connections only. Many devices are set by default to connect automatically to any available wireless signal. The Wi-Fi Alliance recommends changing this setting to require user approval before connecting.
- Disable sharing. Wi-Fi–enabled devices may automatically connect with other devices. File and printer sharing may be common in business and home networks, but avoid this in a public network such as a hotel, restaurant, or airport hot spot.
- Consider additional security measures, such as virtual private networks or firewalls.
- Install a password on personal networks.

`1001110100101010100110010111101101010010101001`

Technology offered a how-to wireless-hacking course that promised to teach students wardriving techniques. In the early days of Wi-Fi, some users considered it a form of public service to share their networks as open nodes for all users, even though such shared use was prohibited by most Internet service providers. Wardriving had the beneficial effect of alerting network users to possible vulnerabilities in their systems, allowing them to take precautions to protect their data. However, not every wardriver acted innocently. The more harmful aspects of wireless hacking included cases involving child pornography downloads and anonymous spam sent by companies and individuals.

The earliest wardrivers logged and collected information about wireless access points without using the networks' services. This is sometimes confused with the practice of connecting to a network and using its services without explicit authorization, more correctly referred to as *piggybacking*. Even when piggybacking occurs unintentionally, it can still be a security threat. Operating systems can be set to connect automatically to any available wireless network. A user who happens to start up a laptop near an access point may find the computer has joined the network without explicit approval. Moreover, a user intending to join one network may instead end up on another one with a stronger signal. This could lead wireless users to inadvertently use an insecure network to log in to a Web site, making their log-in credentials available to anyone listening.

`1001110100101010100110010111101101010010101001`

⊕ Create a personal network name, or service set identifier (SSID), rather than using the default name. This makes the network easy to distinguish from others that may be in the area.

Wireless networks are often the weakest link in a computer system's security because they can be accessed over long distances and without the need to physically access the computer system's hardware. Yet such networks can be secured against all but the most sophisticated hackers by taking relatively simple precautions. Therefore, all computer users should be sure to secure their wireless networks as part of installing such networks to ensure security from the outset and to avoid the need to take complex and costly remedial steps after the network has been breached.

LAPTOPS, SMART PHONES, AND FLASH DRIVES: DATA ON THE MOVE

Increasingly, computer use takes place on the go. People play and shop while traveling, check e-mail from their cars, and work from airplanes. This makes security a particularly challenging problem: People want to stay connected at all times but still maintain control over their data.

This is a particular problem for employers whose workers rely on mobile computing technology. Information technology administrators must ensure that the organization's network is protected from potential compromise from both wandering devices and wandering data. There are many ways for confidential or private data to leave an organization's network. Users may take work home on laptops or copy data to portable storage devices, such as USB flash drives, cell phones, digital cameras, or MP3 players. Data can be intentionally or inadvertently sent via e-mail, which makes it tough to protect against information leakage. The best way to protect the ever-expanding network is to centralize data stores as much as possible, secure devices and USB ports, protect the network with firewalls, and encrypt data. For thorough protection against threats to mobile security, all access points—device, data, user, and network—must be secured to avoid a weak link.

Flash drives, also known as thumb drives or USB keys, pose a particular risk. Because they are great for transporting files and documents back and forth from the office to home or a meeting, the thumb-sized devices have become ubiquitous in schools and workplaces. Their very convenience, however, increases security risks. Flash drives are easy to forget in a computer's USB port, and they are small enough to fall out of—or be taken from—a pocket or bag unnoticed. Also, a computer can become infected with a virus simply by plugging an infected flash drive into its USB port.

A flash drive was blamed in a situation reported in June 2010 at a nuclear power plant in Iran, when a powerful computer virus called the Stuxnet worm targeted the country's Bushehr nuclear power plant and infected computer systems from Asia to Europe and the United States. The malicious software was designed to find a way into a plant's system, where it could steal data or potentially wreak havoc, causing systems such as cooling pumps to malfunction. Cyber security analysts said the virus most likely gained access to systems at the Iranian nuclear power plant through an infected thumb drive. This security threat poses a particular concern for governments and their militaries, because of the many thousands of computers they have spread over vast distances.

To avoid a mobile security crisis, encrypting flash drives is the best practice. This fairly simple process protects files and documents in case the drive falls into the wrong hands. Users can purchase drives that come encrypted out of the box, but they are more expensive. A user with a few minutes can take care of this himself with an encryption utility, such as WinEncrypt, My Lockbox, or EncryptOnClick. A free, open-source solution is offered by a tool called TrueCrypt.

Because mobile computing devices are designed to be portable, they are also vulnerable to plain old low-tech thievery. Take some simple steps to protect laptops while traveling:

- Back up files before leaving home. Even if equipment is lost, the information it contained will be safe.
- Do not use a computer bag that advertises a valuable piece of equipment inside. Instead, use a laptop sleeve for protection and carry it in a tote, traditional briefcase, or other bag.
- Carry laptops on planes instead of checking them with other luggage. If traveling by car, make sure the laptop is out of sight or locked in the trunk before leaving the vehicle.
- Similar to a bike lock, a laptop security cable can attach a laptop to a desk or other heavy piece of furniture in a hotel room or office.
- A portable computer should be set up so a password is required to access the contents. The few seconds it takes to type in the password will be worth the trouble if the computer is stolen. (And of course, one should never keep a written copy of the password with the laptop.)

Some Internet-based services take advantage of the global positioning features contained within many computers and smart phones to make stolen devices easier to track down. Programs such as LocateMyLaptop, Phone Home, or Adeona (which is free) can monitor a lost or stolen computer's location and allow the owner to remotely scramble or delete data.

COMPUTING IN PUBLIC

It may be comfortable and convenient to hang out in the corner coffee shop with a laptop, but computing in public places comes with a host of security risks. Public Wi-Fi networks can be hacked in less than five seconds, according to one study by a British insurance company. From a variety of coffee shops and restaurants, a hacker was able to access more than 350 personal user names and passwords from unsuspecting users in just one hour. The experiment also revealed that more than 200 people made themselves targets by logging in to a fictitious public Wi-Fi network. The study had startling repercussions for home computer security as well. Nearly a quarter of private Wi-Fi networks are set up with no security password, the study found.

Some software developers have turned to scare tactics to warn users about the necessity of safety precautions when using unsecured accounts on popular social networks. Firesheep is one alarming piece of software that makes it possible for a nontechnical person using Mozilla Firefox to easily *sidejack* a nearby Wi-Fi user's Facebook, Twitter, or other unsecured account. The free downloadable add-on was created to scare users into taking safety precautions. Another Web tool, called Idiocy, reveals the security weaknesses inherent in Twitter. Idiocy monitors unsecured Web sessions, such as those on public Wi-Fi networks, and allows a hacker to take control of a user's Twitter account. It then posts a warning message to the user that the account has been hijacked.

If one uses a wireless laptop in coffee shops, libraries, airports, hotels, or other spaces, these tips offer some privacy protection:

- Take advantage of all available protection. If the computer has an up-to-date Windows XP, Windows Vista, or Windows 7 operating system, for instance, it has a built-in firewall that can be configured to provide better protection on a public wireless network.
- Check the privacy statement on the public network's Web site to learn about the type of encryption in use. If it has no privacy statement, consider not using the network.
- Avoid typing in credit card numbers or passwords when using a public wireless network. If this is unavoidable, make sure a locked padlock icon appears at the bottom of the browser window, and make sure the Web address begins with https (the "s" stands for "secure").
- Turn off the wireless network when not in use.

If using a public computer, such as those found in some libraries, airports, or hotel business centers, there are a few additional safety steps:

10011101001010101001100101110110101001010011

Philip Zimmermann, Author of Pretty Good Privacy Encryption Software

Philip Zimmermann is the creator of Pretty Good Privacy, an e-mail encryption software package used by individuals and organizations worldwide.

Born in 1954 in New Jersey, Zimmermann received his bachelor's degree in computer science from Florida Atlantic University in Boca Raton, Florida. He became a software engineer, a job he combined with being a military policy analyst for the Nuclear Weapons Freeze Campaign. During the 1980s, while living in Boulder, Colorado, he became interested in the political aspect of cryptography. Zimmermann taught a class on military policy called "Get Smart in the Arms Race," which focused on nuclear arms development and the effects of the cold war on foreign policy in the Third World.

Zimmermann's involvement with the Union of Concerned Scientists and civil disobedience campaigns in protest of the nuclear arms race twice led to his arrest. In 1991, he became

Philip Zimmermann, creator of the encryption software Pretty Good Privacy (PGP)

concerned with the possibility that Senate Bill 266 might pass. This bill called for manufacturers of secure communications equipment to insert devices that would allow the government to read encrypted messages carried across the networks. Alarmed by the possible erosion of privacy, Zimmermann wrote PGP, intending for it to be used to protect human rights overseas as well as grassroots political

(continues)

10011101001010101001100101110110101001010011

(continued)

movements at home, and published the code on the Internet free of charge. However, PGP quickly spread not only throughout the United States but outside its borders as well. As a result, Zimmermann became a target of a three-year criminal investigation by the U.S. Customs Service, on suspicion that the worldwide spread of PGP violated export restrictions for cryptographic software. Because the government at the time viewed cryptographic software as a munition that could help criminals evade prosecution, it was subject to national security regulations. Even now, exports of cryptographic software are subject to review and licensing requirements by the Department of Commerce.

Zimmermann repeatedly stated that while he took no part in distributing PGP abroad, he believed that a right to encrypt personal communications was a natural extension of the public's reliance on electronic methods as a primary means of communication. He saw e-mail encryption as no different from using an envelope to shield the contents of a letter from prying eyes; denying encryption would be like requiring everyone to use postcards. Governmental control of encrypted electronic communications, he feared, would make anyone who used encryption suspect by default, instead of making protection of private information the status quo. According to Zimmermann, the ability to encrypt electronic communication was a means of safeguarding oneself from undue observation by the government, foreign or domestic. In fact, PGP was relied upon by human rights organizations, journalists, and others all over the globe, especially where free speech was threatened.

- Avoid saving log-on information on a public computer.
- Always log out of Web sites by clicking "log out" on the site. Simply closing the browser window or typing in another address is insufficient.
- Disable features that save user names and passwords.
- Never leave the computer unattended with sensitive information on the screen.
- Erase all tracks. Many browsers offer settings that leave no trace of specific Web activity, or users can simply delete temporary Internet files and history.

At the conclusion of the investigation in early 1996, the U.S. government dropped its case against Zimmermann. Soon after, he testified before the U.S. Senate Committee on Commerce, Science, and Transportation about the need to change export policy for cryptographic software, stressing the need for availability of such software to continue ensuring individual privacy.

Later that year, Zimmermann founded PGP Inc., which was acquired by Network Associates, Inc., in the following year. Zimmermann stayed on as a senior fellow with NAI for three years. In 2002, PGP was bought from NAI by a new company called PGP Corporation, where Zimmermann currently works as a consultant and special adviser. He also consults for a number of companies on matters of cryptography and is a fellow at the Stanford Law School's Center for Internet and Society.

Zimmermann's latest project, the Zfone, provides secure VoIP communications. VoIP differs from the public telephone system because it is vulnerable to an attack on the computer network where it is based. While the public system is relatively difficult to wiretap and that ability is functionally limited to law enforcement, VoIP calls can be compromised by a computer virus. In order to protect the contents of VoIP conversations, Zfone encrypts the conversations using a protocol that sidesteps the phone company. Both parties can verify that no third person is listening in on their conversation, and the information exchange occurs only between them. In contrast, other VoIP encryption protocols rely on servers or the phone company or use public cryptographic keys that can be difficult to manage. Zfone creates a unique key at the beginning of the conversation and destroys it upon completion of the call.

- Be on the lookout for thieves who hover over a user's shoulder to collect sensitive information. A laptop screen guard may prove useful in public situations: The guard slides over the screen, so the user can see the display while directly in front of the computer, but passersby see only a dark, blank screen.

These measures provide some protection against casual hackers, but keep in mind that an industrious thief might have installed sophisticated software on the public computer that records every keystroke and then e-mails that information back to the thief. To really be safe, stick to secure networks and avoid typing credit card numbers or any other financial or otherwise sensitive information into any public computer.

THE INTERNET AS SOAPBOX AND BIG BROTHER

Both governments and those who oppose them make use of computer technology and the Internet. Like the technology traditionally used in publishing and broadcasting, computer and Internet technology are politically neutral, even though they can be used for political purposes by partisans anywhere on the political spectrum to pursue their own ends. There is also the issue that the technology can become a powerful tool for facilitating—or repressing—communication.

In Egypt in early 2011, the government cut off nearly all access to the Internet and shut down cell phone service. The shutdown crippled an important

Egyptian man holds a sign praising Facebook during a protest in Cairo calling for the ouster of Egyptian president Hosni Mubarak in February 2011 *(Khaled Desouki/AFP/Getty Images)*

communications tool being used by antigovernment protesters and their supporters. Activists inside and outside the country of 80 million people worked around the shutdown by using dial-up Internet connections in other countries, faxing eyewitness accounts to overseas friends and relatives, and other means.

Egypt's Internet providers started shutting down their networks at about midnight Cairo time on January 28. Each initiated the process separately, at intervals of two to six minutes. In many countries, including Egypt, access to the Internet is provided by a few large providers that sell service to smaller providers. Most likely, a government official contacted each provider and ordered the service shut off, in response to which one engineer at each provider logged in and changed the traffic flow configuration.

Egypt has only a handful of major Internet access providers, so it would take just a few phone calls to stop the flow of traffic. That would be nearly impossible in countries with larger, more complex networks, such as the United States.

Few governments have cut off access entirely. Myanmar did so in 2007; Nepal two years earlier. But at least 40 countries filter specific Internet sites or services, as China does by prohibiting access to foreign news sources.

Iran was operating one of the world's most sophisticated Web-filtering systems when, in response to street protests following the 2009 presidential election, the government shut down all text messaging. The loss of their prime communication tool led opponents to turn to Twitter and plain old-fashioned word of mouth. Iranian authorities found it easier to limit images and information inside the country than to prevent their spread to the outside world. A loose worldwide network of sympathizers rose up to keep activists connected.

Despite the crackdown, the videos and tweets that flashed across the Web demonstrated that the democratic spirit of young, tech-savvy people could not be completely repressed by an authoritarian government. But while they may have been slow to catch up, governments around the world are turning new Internet tools to their own, antidemocratic purposes.

The very factors that have brought social networking sites such success also have huge appeal for a secret police force. A dissident's social networking and Twitter feed is a handy guide to his political views, career, personal habits, and network of like-thinking friends and relatives. A cybersurfing police officer can compile a dossier on an activist without the trouble of street surveillance or telephone tapping.

When the Iranian revolt collapsed, police followed the electronic trails left by activists to make thousands of arrests. The government even crowd-sourced its hunt for enemies, posting on the Web the photos of unidentified demonstrators and inviting Iranians to identify them.

Further examples include Belarus, where officers of the secret police agency quote activists' comments on Facebook and other sites during interrogations. In Syria, "Facebook is a great database for the government now," Ahed al-Hindi, an exiled Syrian activist who is now with the United States–based group CyberDissidents.org, told a reporter. He believes Facebook is a valuable tool that helps activists form virtual organizations that could never survive otherwise. But he warns users to remember that they are speaking to their oppressors as well as their friends. In China, thousands of commentators are trained and paid to post pro-government comments on the Web and steer online opinion away from criticism of the Communist Party. In Venezuela, President Hugo Chávez, after first denouncing hostile Twitter comments as terrorism, created his own Twitter feed—a strange mix of politics and self-promotion that now has 1.2 million followers.

CONCLUSIONS

A wide variety of technological tools are now available that individuals and organizations can use to protect themselves against attempts to compromise their privacy and security. Such tools are increasingly designed to be used straight out of the box, so that even novice computer users can use them to defend against expert attackers. For better or worse, however, the public availability of such tools means, by definition, that they are available to everyone. Just as human rights activists can use encryption to hide their communications from oppressive governments, so too can oppressive governments use encryption to hide their internal plans from their own populations and the outside world. Just as whistle-blowers can use the Internet to disseminate information about corporate corruption anonymously, so too can criminals use the Internet to plan crimes while evading detection. Every technology that facilitates protecting privacy, security, and anonymity has these two opposing faces.

Some conclude from this that the solution is to ban the use of encryption software and other technologies that can potentially be used for nefarious purposes. However, consider the words of U.S. Supreme Court justice Louis Brandeis (see sidebar in chapter 1) when he famously said in the context of the First Amendment's protection of the right to freedom of speech that, "If there be time to expose through discussion the falsehood and fallacies, to avert the evil by the process of education, the remedy to be applied is more speech, not enforced silence." If Justice Brandeis was correct, then perhaps a corresponding conclusion can be drawn in the context of privacy and security, namely that if technology can be used to invade privacy and violate security, the remedy to be applied is more technology, not suppression of technology.

8

DATABASES, PRIVACY, AND SECURITY: MONITORING THE ONLINE YOU

Everyone uses databases every day, probably without giving them much thought. A database is simply a collection of data stored in an electronic form that is easy to access, modify, sort, and analyze. E-mail programs, online address books, and Internet search engines all use databases. Databases store units of information in *records*. For example, in an address book, each record stores the contact information for a particular person. In turn, each record contains *fields* for storing different kinds of information within the record, such as fields for storing a person's name, address, telephone number, and e-mail address. The number of fields and records that a database may contain is nearly limitless.

In modern society, information about an individual is contained in an array of digital databases. The owners of the databases range from government agencies, such as a state's department of motor vehicles or the federal Social Security Administration, to e-commerce sites of all kinds. Direct marketing providers rely on them, as do credit agencies. Databases are used at schools to store enrollment numbers and grades. Databases track money in bank accounts and inventories in stores. Mobile phone companies use databases to keep track of customer accounts. Hospitals use databases to keep the medical records of their patients. Web sites that provide answers to users' questions use databases to retain questions and their respective answers.

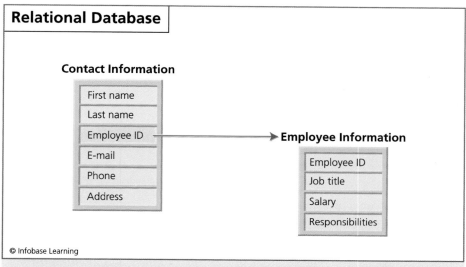

Relational Database

Contact Information

First name
Last name
Employee ID
E-mail
Phone
Address

Employee Information

Employee ID
Job title
Salary
Responsibilities

© Infobase Learning

A database is a collection of data organized into records, where each record contains one or more fields. For example, an address book database may contain one record per person, where each record contains fields for storing the person's first name, last name, e-mail address, telephone number, and mailing address. The collection of all records is stored in a table. A relational database contains multiple tables that are linked to each other. In the example illustrated here, a database includes a contact table (containing contact records) and an employee information table (containing employee information records). The record for a particular person in the contact table does not store all of the details about that person's employment. Instead, such information is stored in a record in the employee information table and is linked to the contact table. One benefit of this scheme is that changes to linked records, such as records in the employee information table, can be made just once and automatically reflected in multiple other tables. Relational databases provide the foundation for almost all commercial databases today.

An electronic address book of the kind described above, which simply contains one record per person, is an example of a *flat file database,* and is analogous to a single set of note cards for storing contact information. Although flat file databases are useful for storing simple collections of data, they are not well-suited to linking different sets of data with each other. As a result, flat file databases are not typically used to store large amounts of data. Instead, most businesses, government agencies, and other entities needing to store complex data sets use *relational databases* to do so. While a flat file database contains only a single set of data—known as a *table*—a relational database contains multiple tables that can be linked to each other. Among the many benefits of relational databases are that they can combine data stored in multiple tables that were originally created separately to effectively create a larger, more complex database, without building it all from scratch. This feature of relational databases also poses potential risks to privacy, because it enables data about people stored in multiple databases to be combined to reveal information about those people which would otherwise have remained hidden.

Many databases containing information about people are created using information provided by those people themselves. People have always offered up various kinds of personal information about themselves, whether by filing a tax return, opening a bank account, or going to the doctor's office. Before computers, all that personal information was relatively secure, because systems based on pieces of paper are so difficult to access, modify, and analyze. Anyone wanting to obtain information from these sources of information would not only need to obtain physical access to all of them, but would also have had to comb through mountains of files stored in many different locations.

In their 1997 book *The Right to Privacy,* Caroline Kennedy and Ellen Alderman describe how the world changed as technology has increasingly become a part of everyday life. They note that most people already have personal infor-

Authors and privacy experts Caroline Kennedy and Ellen Alderman *(Ted Thai/Time Life Pictures/Getty Images)*

mation stored in multiple places, and ever-evolving technology generates even more data. Point-of-sale scanning at a grocery store can create a profile revealing a shopper's preferences. Dashboard-mounted electronic devices allow drivers to whiz through highway toll booths, the toll automatically deducted from their prepaid accounts. These drivers may bypass traffic jams, but they also leave a record of where they were at a particular time.

While concerns about threats to personal privacy dominate the news, consumers also appreciate the convenience of credit cards, automatic teller machines, catalogue shopping, and cellular phones. Many people will happily let the world know which tollbooth they passed through if it means they avoid a traffic jam. In many cases, consumers can apply common sense as they decide what personal information to divulge. An e-commerce Web site collects information such as address, phone numbers, e-mail, and payment accounts to handle a customer's order. The customer is aware of this, since he or she supplied this information when deciding to place the order. Industry best practices require online merchants to store payment accounts and other important identity information on a different computer than the Web site server, so it can be more secure.

Customers may be unaware of all the information that is being gathered each time they visit a Web site. For example, Web sites retain information about customers' preferences to make their shopping experience more personal. Companies also collect information that helps improve their Web sites' technical performance. A good example is the chain of links the user followed to get to their site, all the pages he or she visited on the site, and even which site the user visited next. Online merchants use this information to improve search engine performance or evaluate advertising campaigns. Examining the pages customers visit can help them improve the site's design. Knowing what Web sites users visit next can be of particular interest, especially if the users go straight to a competitor. Another commonly used piece of information is the Internet protocol address of the user's computer. This is useful to help protect the user's identity and prevent fraud. If a user has never before logged in from Ukraine, for example, but someone there is trying to use that person's password and user name, this is a strong indication that someone is attempting to defraud the site.

Much of the information e-commerce sites collect and use is stored right on the user's computer as a cookie, a text file that stores information about individuals' preferences. When someone visits a Web site, the site looks for its own cookies on the user's computer and reads them. Shopping carts are a common use of cookies; the cart keeps track of items the customer put in the cart but did not order. When the customer returns to the site, items placed in the shopping cart on earlier visits are still there. Cookies are used extensively to help customize the browsing experience at most e-commerce Web sites, and computer experts agree that they present little security or identity threat, although they can be used to target advertising at the user.

BENEFITS OF DATABASES

Computers and databases make it possible to gather and store vast amounts of information quickly and easily, which certainly has its benefits. Databases make it possible to run reports summarizing data, thereby making it easy to understand and analyze.

Modern data processing began in 1881, when an engineer named Herman Hollerith tackled the problem of tabulating census data. The Census Bureau, using manual methods, had taken eight years to complete the 1880 census. It was feared that the 1890 count would take even longer. Hollerith invented a device that could automatically read data from a punch card. Later models could sort in addition to adding and featured automatic card punching. Each machine was able to count up to 10,000 items. Hollerith's greatest breakthrough was his use of electricity to read, count, and classify punched cards whose holes represented data collected by the census takers. The machines were used for the 1890 census and accomplished in one year what would have taken 10 years of hand tabulating, saving the Census Bureau $5 million. Hollerith's invention also laid the groundwork for the company that evolved into IBM Corporation.

The move from paper to computer databases was a huge leap in information management and storage. Databases take up less space than paper storage, are easily accessed by multiple users at once, and can be transferred long distances with virtually no delay. The use of databases allowed the rise of corporate infrastructure, credit card processing, e-mail, and the Internet. Databases are used anywhere that data needs to be stored and easily retrieved. Because databases are stored digitally, multiple users in different locations can view the data in more than one place. A bank customer can use any branch for deposits and withdrawals because banks store their customer information and balances in a database. Databases are used to distribute data quickly and easily because they

Gordon Bell, MyLifeBits

Computer pioneer Gordon Bell has turned himself into a living experiment. With the help of fellow researchers, specialized technology, and an assistant dedicated to scanning every piece of paper that relates to his life, he has captured a lifetime's worth of articles, books, cards, CDs, letters, memos, papers, photos, pictures, presentations, home movies, videotaped lectures, and voice recordings and stored them digitally. Like many people, Bell occasionally forgets things. But unlike most people, he can call up his memories on a computer.

Computer engineer Gordon Bell, shown here wearing a Deja View Camwear hands-free video camera as part of his MyLifeBits project, in which he seeks to create and store a complete digital record of his life *(Microsoft Corporation)*

For years, a Microsoft research team has attempted to record all of Bell's communications with other people and machines, as well as the images he sees, the sounds he hears, and the Web sites he visits—storing everything in a personal digital archive that is both searchable and secure. "I'm not particularly interesting," he told one interviewer. "I'm just typical of what you should be able to do."

The project, called *MyLifeBits,* is the digital distillation of, almost literally, Bell's every waking minute. At its heart, MyLifeBits is a big database on a personal computer, into which go the correspondence, keyboard-based chores, and even the sights and sounds of everyday life. It takes in and indexes e-mails, keystrokes, recorded phone calls, images, video, and every Web page that graces its user's computer screen. Bell wears a miniature camera around his neck that snaps away all day. MyLifeBits grabs all those images and the sensor readings too. Just about everything that is digital or that can be digitized goes into the database. If privacy is an overriding concern, MyLifeBits may seem intimidating. But if managing the details of a full and hectic life is a problem, the benefits of the system would be

(continues)

(continued)

undeniable. Countless details, some pivotal, others trivial, could be as easy to call up as the names in an address book.

Bell's full life includes two electrical engineering degrees from the Massachusetts Institute of Technology, two stints at Digital Corporation, and six years teaching computer science at Carnegie Mellon. Then there were two years in the late 1980s as a director at the National Science Foundation, where he led the effort to link the world's supercomputers—the origins of the Internet. He was born in Kirksville, Missouri, in 1934, the son of a grade school teacher and an electrician. In the second grade, Bell developed a heart murmur and spent six months in bed, reading, listening to the radio, and playing with his chemistry set. By age eight, he was working for his father after school. In 1952, Bell became the first person from Kirksville to attend MIT.

In 1945, the engineer and college professor Vannevar Bush set out a blueprint for the electronic age in an *Atlantic Monthly* article. Foremost among its amazingly forward-thinking ideas was a device Bush dubbed the Memex, "A device in which an individual stores all his books, records, and communications, and which is mechanized so that it may be consulted with exceeding speed and flexibility." The 60-year-old vision is a nearly complete description of MyLifeBits. Bush even imagined a compact head-mounted camera and ways of organizing the collection, such as links from one document to another. Brownie cameras, Polaroids, and commercial color film, all developments of the late 1940s, were still several years away.

are only updated once and can be read by many users. A retail chain can see when stores are low in inventory and automatically order more. Prices can be instantly updated across the country.

Securing databases from internal and external snooping is critical to protecting customer data and is one of a company's key competitive assets. If customers lose trust because a business collects unnecessary personal information or fails to protect that information, the bottom line will suffer. The flexibility of databases allows companies to protect sensitive medical or financial data, perhaps by establishing a separate database for this information that is entirely separate from Internet operations. Databases can also be encrypted, stored behind firewalls, and secured in other

For Bell, the project began modestly enough in 1998 when a friend requested electronic copies of some of Bell's books and papers for a digital library project. Using regular desktop scanners and some optical-character-reading software, Bell digitized his own six books, seven patents, and 96 technical articles. This led him to realize that if books could be scanned into a computer, so could all his other files and papers. Documents already in electronic form were funneled in as well, such as e-mail, digital photographs, drafts of articles, even phone bills. His medical records, replete with gene sequences, would eventually get thrown in too. Eventually, every keystroke on his computer would be captured. Office phone calls were not only logged but also digitally recorded. Every Web page Bell viewed was stored. The collection even included a sprawling category he called ephemera, which contained such things as books he has written and books from his library; the labels of bottles of wine he has enjoyed; and the record of a bicycle trip through Burgundy.

Bell's principal collaborator, for the past five years, has been Jim Gemmell, a senior researcher at the Microsoft facility in Redmond, Washington. Aware that they could add to the archive anything they wanted to, Bell and Gemmell began wondering what else they could collect. "We started thinking about Gordon's whole life," Gemmell told one interviewer. "We started going into 'What if I stored everything, what would it mean, what are the implications? We don't know.'" "People argue about the need to forget things," he said, "but if you look at business discipline—advising that you write everything down, your goals and objectives, and return to them to see how you did, examining what went wrong—I think the same thing could happen with our personal lives."

ways. Different levels of access can also be granted to different people. For example, for a medical database, doctors can be given access to patients' prescription history, while receptionists can be limited to viewing dates and times of appointments.

INVASION OF PRIVACY

Increasing use of the Internet generates voluminous flows of personal information from an expanding array of devices. Some uses of personal information are essential to delivering services and applications over the Internet. Others, such

(continues on page 114)

Reidentification: The Challenge of Keeping Data Anonymous

Personal data, such as names and Social Security numbers, can be easily and automatically stripped out of databases to protect people's privacy while still enabling the data to be analyzed and used. This process is called *anonymizing* or de-identification. Computer scientists, however, are finding an increasing variety of ways in which seemingly anonymized data can easily be *reidentified (de-anonymized)*, or linked back to the individuals from whom it came.

In the mid-1990s, the Massachusetts Group Insurance Commission released anonymized data on state employees that showed every single hospital visit made during a certain period. The goal was to help researchers, and the state spent time removing all obvious identifiers, such as name, address, and Social Security number. But a graduate student in computer science saw a chance to make a point about the limits of anonymization. Latanya Sweeney requested a copy of the data and went to work on her reidentification quest. It did not prove difficult. At the time the commission released the data, William Weld, then-governor of Massachusetts, assured the public that patient privacy had been protected. Sweeney started searching for the governor's own hospital records in the insurance data. She knew Governor Weld lived in Cambridge, Massachusetts, a city of 54,000 residents with seven ZIP codes. For 20 dollars, she purchased a database of the complete voter rolls from the city of Cambridge. This gave her the name, address, ZIP code, birthdate, and sex of every voter. By combining this data with the hospital records, Sweeney found Governor Weld with ease. Only six people in Cambridge shared his birthdate, only three of them were men, and of them, only he lived in his zip code.

Such work by computer scientists has shown a serious flaw in the basic idea behind the concept of personally identifying information—almost all information can be personal when combined with enough other relevant bits of data. This was the idea behind a somewhat controversial experiment conducted by two MIT students in a class on ethics and law on the electronic frontier. Using data from Facebook, they made a striking discovery: Just by looking at a person's online friends, they could predict with a high degree of accuracy whether the person was gay. The project, dubbed "Gaydar" by the students, examined

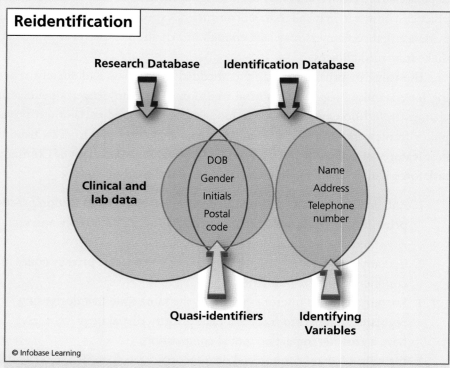

Reidentification

Research Database   Identification Database

Clinical and
lab data

DOB
Gender
Initials
Postal
code

Name
Address
Telephone
number

Quasi-identifiers   **Identifying
Variables**

© Infobase Learning

Reidentification (also called de-anonymization) is the process of identifying the person who is associated with data that are intended to be anonymous. For example, if a medical patient's name and Social Security number have been stripped from the patient's electronic medical record, it still may be possible to identify the name and Social Security number of the patient by correlating information in the electronic medical record with information in other databases, such as employment databases and automobile registration databases.

what the connections between people reveal. The program correctly guessed the sexual orientation of 10 men who were known to be homosexual but did not explicitly reveal it on Facebook. Although the sample was very small, the findings made sense: People network and relate to people with whom they have something in common. From there, a little data mining can easily reveal all sorts of things about a person.

(continued from page 111)
as personalized advertising, support the digital economy. Some commercial data practices, however, may fail to meet consumers' expectations of privacy. There is evidence that consumers may lack enough information about these practices to make informed choices.

The value of privacy is deeply embedded in U.S. law and society, reflecting long-standing legal and cultural traditions. But many experts believe that changes in technology and business models have rendered parts of our privacy policy framework out of date. To address new challenges and to draw from the best features of current privacy law and policy, a U.S. Department of Commerce task force issued policy recommendations in four broad categories:

1. Enhance consumer trust online through use of fair information practice principles, guidelines that represent widely accepted privacy and security standards for an electronic marketplace.
2. Encourage the development of voluntary, enforceable privacy codes of conduct in specific industries.
3. Encourage global interoperability. At the same time that decreasing regulatory barriers to trade is a high priority, disparate privacy laws have a growing impact on global competition.
4. Institute a federal commercial data security breach notification law that sets national standards, addresses inconsistent state laws, and authorizes enforcement.

Other consumer protections are in place as well. Online merchants that accept credit card payment are required to comply with the *Payment Card Industry Data Standards (PCI DSS)*. PCI is an organization formed by the major payment card brands—American Express, Discover Financial Services, JCB, MasterCard Worldwide, and Visa Inc. The standards define best practices for securing payment account data and other personal information. However, compliance with these standards remains the responsibility of the merchant, and participants perform their own compliance and enforcement assessments.

In spite of national attention to privacy standards and steps taken by reputable online merchants and e-commerce providers, personal information can sometimes be compromised. In December 2010, McDonald's reported that some of its customers' private information may have been accessed during a data breach. A third party was able to bypass security measures and gain access to a database of customer information that included e-mail and other contact information, birthdates and other specifics. Customers provided this information when they signed up for online promotions or other subscriptions to its Web sites. In January 2011, the University of Connecticut warned thousands of customers who bought items on its HuskyDirect.com Web site that their personal information may have been exposed in a data security breach. The information at risk included customers' names, addresses, e-mail, telephone numbers, credit card numbers, expiration dates, and security codes. Those affected were notified, and the university arranged for credit protection for those customers.

Some companies create their own privacy problems. In 2003, JetBlue secretly gave personal information on some 5 million passengers to a private contractor who was working on a data-mining project for the Bush administration. The contractor merged the airline's database with Social Security numbers, home addresses, income levels, and vehicle ownership information it purchased elsewhere. JetBlue faced lawsuits over the apparent breach of its privacy policy, which assured its Web customers that "financial and personal information collected on this site is not shared with any third parties."

DENIAL OF OPPORTUNITY

Internet behavior, from clicks on banner advertisements to specific Google searches, is tracked in various ways, whether or not users have any direct notification from those doing the tracking. This phenomenon becomes especially apparent when Web ads seem to know an individual's shopping habits, relationship statuses, and other identifying data. This practice, known as *data profiling,* is often employed by Internet marketers, who purchase information about consumers' online activity to deliver effective, targeted ad campaigns just for them. Although not nefarious on its face, the use of data profiling can lead to discrimination, or *denial of opportunity,* in the workplace, marketplace, or health care.

In the 1960s and 1970s, the practice of *redlining* was common in the United States. Banks and other businesses placed real estate markets into socioeconomic, racial, and other demographic categories. Redlining prevented residents of certain neighborhoods from receiving mortgage loans, persuaded retailers to establish their businesses in more affluent areas, and encouraged the denial of employment, insurance, health care, and other essential services to individuals and families based purely on where they lived. Redlining is outlawed today, but a similar practice, called *weblining,* still exists online. It can be used both to promote services to one type of demographic and to deemphasize the same services to another. Weblining occurs as a direct result of data profiling, which aggregates a rich series of personal, Internet-based information to determine exactly who a user is. Though difficult to prove and the subject of only a handful of lawsuits, weblining means that certain individuals will have less access to—and possibly pay more for—some products and services than others.

Another form of discrimination can deny someone a job, medical care, or medical insurance based on the person's genetic predisposition to have a disease. Such information can be obtained from DNA databases, which are becoming increasingly common. *Genetic tests,* while potentially valuable for medical treatment, produce data that can be used to discriminate against patients. An increasing number of healthy individuals have suffered as a result, as in these cases documented by the Council for Responsible Genetics:

- Danny, age 7, is healthy, but testing reveals a gene predisposing him to a heart disorder. Even though he takes medication that lowers his risk of a heart attack, he is denied health insurance. His insurance company argues that the presence of the gene is a preexisting medical condition.
- Suspecting her young son has a learning disability, Lisa consults her doctor. Genetic testing reveals that Jonathan has fragile X syndrome, an inherited form of mental retardation. Their insurance company cancels Jonathan's health coverage, claiming that his disability represents a preexisting condition. Lisa searches unsuccessfully for another company that will insure her son. She ultimately quits her job to qualify for Medicaid.
- Kim is a social worker. During a staff workshop on caring for people with chronic illnesses, she mentions that her mother died of Huntington's disease. Kim herself has a 50 percent chance of developing this fatal genetic condition. One week after she reveals her risk status, Kim is fired—even though her performance record is exemplary.

Not only is this discrimination unjust, it is scientifically inaccurate. Genes tell only part of the story about why some people get sick and others do not.

Even if researchers could know exactly what genes a person has, they still would be unable to predict their future health needs. This is because many genetic tests predict—with limited accuracy—that a disease may develop at an undetermined time in the future. Because the severity of many diseases—such as sickle cell anemia and spina bifida—varies widely among individuals, a genetic prediction cannot foretell how disabling the disease will be for a specific person.

The *Americans with Disabilities Act (ADA)* of 1990 forbids employers from discriminating against disabled individuals who are able to perform their duties with reasonable accommodation. In revised guidelines released in March 1995, the Equal Employment Opportunities Commission (EEOC) stated that healthy individuals who have a genetic predisposition to a disease and are thus perceived as disabled fall within the scope of the ADA. There is no valid justification for employers to perform mandatory DNA testing on their employees, since they are forbidden by the ADA from using this information in employee evaluations.

Genetic databases in many areas have become magnets for controversy. For instance, privacy law experts predict that eventually most citizens in Great Britain will be linked to data stored in the police's DNA database. The police are allowed to retain DNA data on those arrested even if those people are not charged or convicted. Data from these samples are then added to the National DNA Database. The practice has been slowed by lawsuits but still continues.

The University of California, Berkeley, began asking incoming students in the spring of 2010 to voluntarily provide DNA samples. The data was to be used to track students' ability to tolerate alcohol, absorb folic acid, and metabolize lactose. Students were to be provided with a Web site through which they could check their results using an anonymous bar code. The intent of the program was to inform students if they should eat more vegetables, for instance, or limit their alcohol intake. The goal of the program was not to identify potentially danger-ous genes, but to point out traits that could be managed through behavior. After receiving numerous complaints about the program, however, the California Department of Public Health instructed the university not to permit students to see their personal results. Instead, the university was permitted only to present the results in aggregate to the student body through lectures and panel discus-sions. The basis for the department's decision was that the program as originally designed would need to comply with laws intended to ensure the accuracy and quality of diagnostic tests used in providing medical care to patients and that the university had not taken the steps necessary to certify that the program complied with such laws. As this case illustrates, the mere fact that certain kinds of genetic tests are becoming increasingly easy to use does not necessarily mean that such tests can lawfully be provided in any manner desired by the entity providing the test.

There is a world of information out there, and human resources departments and college admissions officials are using it to guide their decisions. A Microsoft survey found that 79 percent of human resources professionals surveyed in the United States reported reviewing such information when examining potential job candidates. The information makes a difference: 70 percent of hiring managers in the study said they have rejected candidates based on what they found. Likewise, a good online reputation has become part of a successful college application. More and more, colleges and universities are using information posted online to rank applicants.

These developments make it even more surprising that the gap between people's actual and perceived online behavior is widening. In the same survey, 83 percent of consumers polled said they believe they have some control over their online reputation. But less than half of them consider their reputation every time they post information. Only 32 percent consider the reputations of others. People may not fully realize how that information can be used, one Microsoft official noted. More than a third of respondents said they are not concerned that their online reputation may affect their personal or professional lives and almost half said they believe it is inappropriate for potential employers to review job candidates' online photos and videos.

HOW TO PROTECT ONESELF

While many people do take action to help protect their online reputations, such efforts are largely limited to blocking access to online profiles and other data. Fewer users take more proactive measures, such as regularly running their own names through a search engine; using alert features to find new information; or contacting a Web site owner or administrator to remove false or derogatory content. Web content is accessible to anybody who searches for it, and information can be interpreted in ways the user never intended. Online content can surface even years after being posted.

A user can monitor his or her online presence and assess the impression it leaves on people by following these steps:

- **Search by name.** Begin by typing one's first and last name into several popular search engines to see where one is mentioned and in what context. If the user has ever used a different name, uses a middle name or initial, uses a nickname, or if the name is frequently misspelled, search all variations.
- **Focus the search.** To get more precise results, put quotation marks around the name, so the search engine reads it as a phrase and not as two or more unrelated words. If others share the same name, eliminate many false hits by adding keywords that apply only to the individual, such as hometown, employer, or a hobby.
- **Expand the search.** Use similar techniques to search for telephone numbers, home address, e-mail addresses, and personal Web site domain names. Also search for Social Security and credit card numbers to make sure they don't appear anywhere online.
- **Target specific sites.** Check online phone directories, genealogy sites, alumni sites, the Web sites of organizations to which the user belongs, and other sites that compile personal, professional, or contact information about people.
- **Read blogs.** If any friends, family members, or coworkers have blogs or personal Web pages on social networking sites, check them out to see if they are writing about or posting pictures of the user.
- **Sign up for alerts.** Use the feature provided by some search engines that automatically notifies the user of any new mention of his or her name or other personal information.

If the search turns up negative information, take steps to eliminate or reduce it. Contact the Web site owner or administrator and ask them to remove it. Most sites have policies to deal with such errors. If the poster is a friend or classmate, talk to them and ask them to remove the information. Failing this, commercial online privacy services may be able to provide professional-strength solutions.

Users can also take preventive action by limiting the amount and kind of private data that they make available online:

- **Safeguard personal information.** Keep personal information private online. Be equally careful about sharing information offline and know how organizations will use private information before giving it to them.
- **Use privacy settings.** Most social networking and photo-sharing sites allow users to limit who can access and respond to content.
- **Don't mix public and private lives online.** Use different e-mail addresses for different online activities to help keep public and private lives separate.
- **Choose photos thoughtfully.** Whether the user is a child or an adult, make sure potential colleges or employers cannot search the Web and find questionable images.
- **Watch language and content.** Always assume that anyone can read anything one has written online.

Users can also limit the ways in which owners of databases can share information about them with others. To prevent sensitive data from ending up in the wrong hands:

- **Limit the information shared on Web sites.** For example, if a user logs in to Yahoo! only to read and send e-mail, there is no need to have a robust, comprehensive Yahoo! profile. In fact, the only required information the user needs to provide is full name and display name, both of which can and should be set to private.
- **Beware of fan pages.** In the early days of Facebook, becoming a fan of a certain band or company was a fun and easy way for users to tell friends what they liked and keep up with the latest news. In reality, fanning or liking a page on Facebook or, worse yet, authorizing an unfamiliar application, can sometimes give the owner access to the user's personal data. Users should be careful what they like.
- **Log out before surfing.** Whether on e-mail, Facebook, LinkedIn, online banking, or any other account that contains personal information, it is always a good idea to log out before browsing the Internet. If possible, open up a new browser window, or better, a different Internet browser altogether before conducting a search. A third-party application, such as TrackMeNot, can also be used to prevent Internet

marketers and data profilers from obtaining data or tracking search habits. TrackMeNot and other similar programs install directly into the Internet browser and conduct random searches that act as red herrings for data profiling programs, resulting in a highly inaccurate account of the user's online activity. Other services, such as Anonymizer, ensure Internet privacy by concealing the user's IP address.

- **Follow general safety guidelines.** When buying online, find out how personal information will be used and whether it will be shared with others. Research the company's privacy policy—how will it use and protect personal information? Use a secure browser and put passwords on all accounts. Avoid using easily available information, such as a relative's name, one's birthdate, or one's phone number, or obvious choices, such a series of consecutive numbers or one's hometown football team. Keep password information in a safe, private place.

Sometimes even the most careful user can fall prey to Internet predators. Having one's information lost or stolen can be a frightening experience, causing worries about how the information may be misused if it falls into the wrong hands. Fortunately, if one's data may have been accessed without authorization, there are ways to detect misuse that has already occurred and to help prevent potential future misuse:

- If the stolen information includes financial accounts, close compromised credit card accounts immediately. Consult with the user's financial institution about whether to close bank or brokerage accounts immediately or first change passwords and have the institution monitor for possible fraud. Place strong passwords on any new accounts.
- If the stolen information includes the user's Social Security number, call the toll-free fraud number of any one of the three nationwide consumer reporting companies and register an initial fraud alert. This alert can help stop someone from opening new credit accounts in the user's name.
- If a company experiences a breach the company may offer free credit monitoring. Consider accepting this offer, as credit monitoring from

(continues on page 124)

Simson L. Garfinkel, Author, Database Security Expert

Simson Garfinkel has been an associate professor at the Naval Postgraduate School in Monterey, California, since 2006. His research interests lie in the field of computer forensics, document and media exploitation, personal information management, usability and security, and information policy and terrorism. Garfinkel received three bachelor of science degrees from the Massachusetts Institute of Technology in 1987 (chemistry, political science, and a degree from the Program in Science, Technology and Society), a master's degree from the Columbia School of Journalism in 1988, and a doctorate in computer science and engineering from MIT in 2005. Through August 2008 he was a fellow at the Center for Research on Computation and Society at Harvard University.

In 1995, Garfinkel cofounded Vineyard.NET, the first Internet service provider on Martha's Vineyard, launched with $5,000 in personal investment. Vineyard.NET was purchased in 2000 by a wireless Internet service provider that later went bankrupt, enabling Garfinkel to repurchase the company in bankruptcy court. He is also a founder of Sandstorm Enterprises, a computer security firm developing advanced computer forensic audit tools used by businesses and governments.

In addition to his academic and business career, Garfinkel is a contributing writer to several publications and writes an award-winning monthly column on computer security for *CSO* magazine, where he is also an editor. He is a contributing editor at *Technology Review* magazine and writes a weekly emerging technology blog. The blog entries focus on various issues in computer security and privacy as well as the ways both can be compromised. Garfinkel frequently conducts personal research on the topics he writes about. For example, for a piece that discussed refurbished computer hard drives being sold with original data still present, Garfinkel bought his own refurbished hard drives on the Internet and discovered that about a third of them did in fact contain personal data. That research project, which also became part of Garfinkel's doctoral dissertation, was completed with Abhi Shelat. About a third of all drives they purchased were properly wiped, a third were broken, and a third still contained the owner's files. Following a suggestion from a friendly computer forensics specialist, Garfinkel was able to salvage the data from some of the broken hard drives by placing

Simson Garfinkel, computer researcher and database security expert, shown here holding one of more than 100 used hard disk drives that he purchased, most of which still contained personal data about their previous owners (*AP Images*)

them overnight in a freezer. Along with reports of hard drives of computers sent for repair making their way into the public domain, this experiment caused Garfinkel to suggest that instead of offering warranties that include hard drive repair, computer manufacturers should focus on making hard drives cheap and easily replaceable to minimize data theft. Incidentally, he observed a decline in the number of refurbished hard drives containing personal information in the years after his research findings were published.

Garfinkel details another personal experience in which his graduate school application information, including Social Security number, were published online as a consequence of a school computer containing his application data being decommissioned but not destroyed. Another entry points out a security flaw in Lojack for Laptops antitheft software, which proved to be completely ineffective if a stolen computer underwent clean reinstallation of the operating system.

(continues)

001101010010100111010110101010101100101000001

(continued)

Garfinkel has also written about the vulnerability of relying on Social Security numbers for identity verification and the ease with which they can be compromised, either through social engineering or simply by obtaining improper records on an individual.

Garfinkel is an author or coauthor of 14 books on computing, including *Database Nation: The Death of Privacy in the 21st Century,* and *Practical UNIX and Internet Security* (coauthored with Gene Spafford). He is also an FAA licensed pilot.

001101010010100111010110101010101100101000001

(continued from page 121)

a reputable company can help quickly detect any misuse of personal information.

- If the stolen information includes the user's driver's license or other government-issued identification, contact the agencies that issued the documents and follow their procedures to cancel a document and get a replacement. Ask the agency to flag the file to keep anyone else from getting a license or another identification document under false pretenses.

- Watch for signs that private information is being misused. For example, certain bills or other mail may not arrive on time. Follow up with creditors. A missing bill could mean an identity thief has taken over an account and changed the billing address to cover his tracks. Other signs include receiving credit cards that one did not apply for; being denied credit for no apparent reason; and receiving calls or letters from debt collectors or businesses about merchandise or services one did not buy.

If one's information has been misused, file a report about the identity theft with the police and file a complaint with the Federal Trade Commission at www.ftc.gov/idtheft. Also, many states have laws that govern how businesses should respond to data breaches and what notice or assistance they are required to provide to affected consumers.

CONCLUSIONS

Maintaining privacy and security in the face of increasingly vast databases containing information about nearly every aspect of people's lives are perhaps the most challenging problems today. As this chapter illustrates, it is not enough to strip personally identifying information from a single database, because such information can often be reconstructed by correlating the information in multiple databases. Furthermore, there is an inherent tension between limiting access to databases and the need to grant access to databases so that they can be used for their intended purposes. Even if access to a particular database is successfully limited to the appropriate set of people, any leakage of such data can enable new databases to be created with the same information. Once such additional databases exist, the data they contain can almost never be made secure again, because the further spread of the data cannot be stopped. This problem is exacerbated by the common use of a limited set of information, such as the names, Social Security numbers, and driver's license numbers, to identify people across a wide variety of databases.

Strengthening existing laws protecting personal privacy and requiring owners of databases to maintain the security of them would help to address the problem. So too would restricting the range of uses to which individual databases are put and restricting the use of Social Security numbers as universal personal identifiers. Yet perhaps the most promising pathways for protecting the privacy and security of databases lie in ongoing technological developments in encryption, biometrics (such as fingerprint readers and eye scanners), and software for monitoring patterns in database access to detect suspicious activity. Although none of these can yet be guaranteed to solve the serious threats to privacy and security that databases pose, they promise to create increased demand for a generation of computer engineers and programmers who are up to the challenge.

CHRONOLOGY

1760   King George II dies; all existing writs of assistance were due to terminate six months after his death

Massachusetts colonists led by James Otis unsuccessfully challenge the issuance of new writs of assistance

1889   Herman Hollerith is issued a patent for his Electric Tabulating System, which uses punched cards to numerically encode data

1945   Vannevar Bush publishes an article in the *Atlantic Monthly* that describes his concept of the memex, an electromechanical device that could be used to create and store notes and link to notes created by others; though never realized, his idea prefigured hypertext on the Internet

1965   The U.S. Supreme Court rules in *Griswold v. Connecticut* that the U.S. Constitution protects the right to privacy; the case centered on an individual's right to use birth control

1967   The U.S. Supreme Court rules in *Katz v. United States* that the right of privacy prohibits eavesdropping in the form of wiretaps by law enforcement officials

1970   E. F. Codd, a researcher at IBM, invents the relational database

1974   Robert Ellis Smith begins publishing the *Privacy Journal* newsletter

1982   Kevin Mitnick hacks into the North American Air Defense Command computer system

1986   U.S. Congress passes the Electronic Communications Privacy Act (ECPA) to limit the ways in which law enforcement can access electronic data stored and transmitted by computers

(c)Brain, the first widespread computer virus, is released

1988   Robert Morris releases his experimental Morris worm

1989   John McAfee founds antivirus company McAfee Associates

1991   Philip Zimmermann creates Pretty Good Privacy (PGP), an encryption and decryption program used to protect the privacy of data communication

1994   Electronic Privacy Information Center (EPIC) is founded by David Banisar, Marc Rotenberg, and David Sobel

1996   The U.S. Health Insurance Portability and Accountability Act (HIPAA) is enacted by Congress to regulate the use and disclosure of medical records

1998   Congress passes the Identity Theft and Assumption Deterrence Act, prohibiting identity theft

1999   Melissa, the first worldwide e-mail virus, is released

2000   ILOVEYOU virus infects more than 50 million computers and causes an estimated $5–$10 billion in damages

Children's Online Privacy Protection Act (COPPA) of 1998 goes into effect, requiring Web site operators to protect children's safety and privacy online

2001   USA PATRIOT (United and Strengthening America by Providing Appropriate Tools Required to Intercept and Obstruct Terrorism) Act is enacted by U.S. Congress in response to terrorist attacks on September 11

Code Red virus attempts an attack on the official White House Web site; Code Red II, a second version of the virus, causes an estimated $2 billion in damages

Nimbda computer worm becomes the most widespread virus or worm on the Internet

2004   MyDoom becomes the fastest-spreading e-mail worm in history

Thieves attempt to use keylogging spyware to steal over $200 million from Sumitomo Mitsui Banking Corporation

2005 LexisNexis information service reports a security breach affecting the personal records of more than 310,000 people

2006 Social Security numbers for 26.5 million veterans are compromised when a laptop computer and external drive are stolen from the home of a Department of Veterans Affairs employee

2008 Conficker worm is identified; by 2010 it is believed to control more than 7 million computers around the world

Sony is fined $1 million by the FTC for collecting personal information from more than 30,000 children on their entertainment Web sites and allowing children to interact online with adults

2009 A series of coordinated cyber attacks target major news media, government, and financial Web sites in the United States and South Korea; the attacks were discovered to have been triggered by the activation of a botnet

The Daprosy worm is detected; the worm, which logs keystrokes, is spread through e-mail and removable mass storage devices

CareerBuilder.com, the largest online job listing Web site in the United States, reports that roughly half of employers use social media sites like Facebook to screen job applicants

An estimated 11.2 million people are estimated to have been victims of identity theft and related fraud at a cost of about $54 billion

2010 Albert Gonzalez is sentenced to 20 years in prison in connection with the largest identity theft case in U.S. history; Gonzalez led an international ring that stole more than 40 million credit card and debit card records from major retailers

Stuxnet computer worm attacks Siemens SCADA industrial equipment; the worm is the most complex and potentially dangerous in history and is believed to have targeted the Iran nuclear program

Intel, the world's largest computer chip manufacturer, purchases antivirus company McAfee for $7.7 billion

The U.S. Cybersecurity Act of 2010, which would provide the federal government with more power to control the information infrastructure when national security is at issue, is passed by a Senate committee and goes before Congress

Online poker network Cereus makes itself vulnerable to hackers by using a weak encryption method to display sensitive client information

Facebook rolls out changes to security settings that make previously private data public

2011   Hackers breach Sony's PlayStation Network and Qriocity online music and film service, providing access to 23,400 credit and debit card records and personal account information of 24.6 million account holders

GLOSSARY

adware   software that tracks a computer user's Internet browsing habits and displays targeted pop-up and banner advertisements

Americans with Disabilities Act (ADA) of 1990   a civil rights law that prohibits discrimination based on an individual's disability

anonymizing   the process of stripping personal data such as names and Social Security numbers out of databases while still allowing the remaining data to be analyzed and used (also known as **de-identification**)

antivirus software   software used to protect a computer from viruses, worms, Trojan Horses, spyware, adware, and other types of malware

black hat hackers   computer security term used to describe people who develop malicious software (see **white hat hackers**)

bomb   a computer virus designed to execute on a specific date or when a specific event or action occurs

boot sector   the area of a hard disk, floppy disk, or other storage device that contains code for starting software programs, including the computer's operating system program

boot sector virus   a computer virus that infects the boot sector of a storage device

botnet   a network of computers that have been infected by malware and are acting under the command of controlling software

browser hijacker   spyware that replaces an Internet user's home page and redirects Internet searches to an unexpected Web site

bug   a flaw in a computer program that causes it to behave unexpectedly

cipher   in cryptography, an algorithm for performing encryption or decryption

cloud-based services   computer services that are delivered over the Internet rather than by a user's personal computer or a server within the user's organization

130

computer virus a software program that is designed to attack individual computers or computer networks

con man a swindler who operates by gaining the confidence of his **mark,** or victim; short for confidence man

cookie a text file placed on a computer's hard drive by a Web browser; cookies usually contain information about a user's preferences and Web site settings

cryptography writing in secret code

database an organized collection of data usually stored in digital form on a computer; information in a database is easy to access, modify, sort, and analyze

data miner spyware that gathers information about a computer user

data profiling the practice of using information gathered from a user's Web activities to deliver targeted advertising

de-anonymizing (reidentifying) the process of restoring identifying personal data that has been stripped from a database by anonymizing

decryption the process of returning encrypted data to its original form, so that it can be understood by a human (see **encryption**)

denial of opportunity unfair treatment due to bias or prejudice

dialup spyware spyware that changes a computer's dialup connection setting so that computer calls are directed to a phone number which charges the caller

digital certificate a unique piece of code or a large number that verifies that a Web server is trusted by an independent source known as a certificate authority

digitization conversion of analog information such as text, photographs, or audio recordings into a digital format that can be stored and transmitted electronically

drive-by download spyware installation that takes place without a computer user's permission when the user clicks on a webpage link

drone a computer that has been infected by malware that causes it to act under the command of controlling software (also known as a **bot** or **zombie bot**)

Dumpster diving scavenging for information from commercial or residential trash containers; a hacker may use information obtained from discarded trash to carry out a computer network attack

encryption the conversion of data into a form that cannot be easily understood by unauthorized users (see **decryption**)

end-user license agreement (EULA) a software license agreement that is usually displayed on a computer monitor with a button that the user must click to accept the terms of the license before the user is allowed to install and/or use software or access a Web site

field a specific unit of information stored in a database record (see **record**)

firewall a computer component that blocks unauthorized network access to the computer; a firewall may consist of hardware, software, or a combination of the two

flash drive a flash memory data storage device that connects to a computer via an integrated Universal Serial Bus (USB) interface (also referred to as **USB flash drive**)

flat file database a simple database that stores information in a single table of records

freeware free software; some freeware is the source of surreptitious spyware

general warrant an official document issued by a government that allows law enforcement officials to perform a broad search without stating the person or place to be searched or the objects being sought

genetic tests tests performed on blood and other tissues to find genetic disorders

Googlewash Internet slang for an attempt to influence the Google search engine ranking of a given page (also referred to as a **Google bomb**)

grifter a swindler who uses confidence or deception to defraud others

hyperlink a word, phrase, or image on a webpage that can be clicked on to jump to a new webpage or a new location within the same webpage

London scam   a social networking confidence scheme that tricks people into sending money after receiving an e-mail that appears to be from a friend who claims to be stranded in London with no way home

loyaltyware   a benign form of spyware that rewards customer loyalty by awarding points, airline miles, or some other prize to shoppers who make purchases from targeted Web sites

macro   a small piece of programming code that is embedded in a word processing document or spreadsheet

macro virus   a computer virus that is embedded in a document or spreadsheet macro

malware   software that has been designed with malicious intent

mark   the victim of a confidence scheme (see **con man**)

memex   a device envisioned by Vannevar Bush in the 1930s that could be used to store notes and link to notes created by others; though never realized, his idea prefigured hypertext on the Internet

microfilm   film containing reduced reproductions of printed materials for easy storage and transmission

MyLifeBits   a Microsoft Research project inspired by Vannevar Bush's theoretical **memex** device; the subject of the project is computer scientist Gordon Bell, whose life is being preserved through digital storage

Nigerian scam   a confidence scheme that uses e-mails promising large rewards in exchange for a small investment

password cracker   software that decrypts passwords or otherwise obtains passwords without the permission of their owners

payload   the portion of a virus program that is intended to harm an infected computer

Payment Card Industry Data Security Standard (PCI DSS)   an international credit card standard that helps prevent credit card fraud

peer-to-peer (P2P)   a system that allows users of a network to share files directly between computers without using an intermediate server

pen register a surveillance device that is attached to a telephone line and records all dialed numbers

personally identifying information (PII) information that can be used to identify a person or can be combined with other data to identify a person

phishing attempting to acquire private information, such as passwords or credit card numbers, using e-mail or Web sites that appear to be legitimate

piggybacking connecting to a network and using its services without explicit authorization

piracy illegal use and distribution of copyrighted software

plug-in a software component that provides additional functionality to an existing application such as a Web browser

Ponzi scheme a fraudulent investment scheme that pays investors with money taken from other investors rather than from legitimate investments; if undetected, the scheme eventually fails when the amount owed to investors surpasses the amount taken from new investors

Pretty Good Privacy (PGP) an encryption and decryption program used to protect the privacy of data communication

program virus a computer virus that infects executable files

public key encryption (also known as asymmetric key encryption) a data encryption scheme that uses both a public key and a private key; the use of two keys that are not shared between sender and receiver provides very secure encryption

record a unit of information in a database; a record contains **fields** for storing different types of information

redlining a now-illegal practice from the 1960s and 1970s that prevented residents of certain neighborhoods from receiving mortgage loans and encouraged the denial of employment, insurance, health care, and other essential services to individuals and families based purely on where they lived

relational database a complex database that contains multiple tables of records that can be linked to each other

right to privacy   the right to be left alone; many consider this right to extend to an individual's body, thoughts, home, and identity

RSA   an algorithm used for Internet encryption and authentication; used by Web browsers from Microsoft and Netscape

screen name   a name chosen to be used when communicating with others online

search engine   computer technology that finds and retrieves information that satisfies some criteria; commonly refers to Web-based applications that search the Internet for webpages that contain specified words

security through obscurity (STO)   a principle of security engineering that relies on keeping the internals of a system secret in order to provide security; most security experts consider STO to be inferior to other forms of security

shoulder surfing   using direct observation (such as looking over someone's shoulder when they enter a password) to obtain information to be used to break into a computer network

sidejacking   remotely hijacking another user's Web session by intercepting and using credentials that identified the user to the session server

social engineering   a type of fraud that gains an individual's trust in order to trick the individual into revealing secure information

spam advertising   the use of electronic messaging systems such as e-mail to send unsolicited bulk advertising

spyware   software that surreptitiously tracks a computer user's keystrokes and mouse clicks

SSL (Secure Sockets Layer)   an encryption protocol used to transmit private information over the Internet; used by both Microsoft Mozilla, and Apple Web browsers

subpoena   a writ (written order), usually issued by a court, that compels a witness to give testimony or produce evidence

table   a single set of data in a database

Trojan horse a software program that appears to perform a useful function but is actually malicious

Universal Serial Bus (USB) a connection standard that allows computer peripheral devices (such as keyboards, printers, and flash drives) to connect to a host controller (usually a personal computer)

wardriving picking up wireless signals from a building by driving near it

warez copyrighted works that are distributed in violation of copyright laws; P2P file sharing is often used to share warez

weblining an Internet practice, similar to **redlining,** that is used to promote services to one type of demographic and to deemphasize the same services to another

white hat hackers computer security term used to describe people who expose and create antidotes for malicious software (see **black hat hackers**)

Wi-Fi Alliance a trade association that certifies Wireless LAN technology

Wi-Fi Protected Access II (WPA2) a wireless security protocol and certification program developed by the Wi-Fi Alliance

Wired Equivalent Privacy (WEP) one of the earliest wireless encryption standards

worm a malicious program that can replicate without human interaction by sending copies of itself to computers on a network

writ of assistance a general warrant that allowed customs officials to perform searches for smuggled contraband without specific details; once issued, this type of warrant remained valid as long as the sovereign who signed it was alive and for an additional six months following his death

zombie bot a computer that has been infected by malware that causes it to act under the command of controlling software (also known as a **drone**)

FURTHER RESOURCES

The following resources are arranged according to chapter title.

"Your Right to Privacy"

BOOKS

Pfaffenberger, Bryan. *Protect Your Privacy on the Internet.* Hoboken, N.J.: John Wiley & Sons, 1997. Teaches Internet users the programs and settings they need to keep their information private and protect online transactions.

ARTICLES

Boettger, Larry. "Protecting Data Privacy on School Computer Systems." Inside the School Web site. Available online. URL: http://www.insidetheschool.com/articles/protecting-data-privacy-on-school-computer-syste ms/. Accessed July 5, 2011. Preventing hackers from gaining access to school networks is difficult because school districts often do not have the money to secure their networks. Students and teachers should follow several steps from the article to ensure that their data remains private.

Lattanzio, Vince. "WebcamGate Teen: I Hope They're Not Watching Me." NBC Philadelphia Web site. Available online. URL: http://www.nbcphiladelphia.com/news/local-beat/WebcamGate-Teen-I-Hope-Theyre-Not-Wat ching-Me-84826357.html. Accessed July 5, 2011. The students at the center of the controversy over school access to privately issued laptops speak out.

"Leading Article: In Search of Online Privacy." Independent Web site. Available online. URL: http://www.independent.co.uk/opinion/leading-articles/leading-article-in-search-of-online-privacy-806284.html. Accessed July 5, 2011. Google fights the European Union, arguing that data retention is essential to the functionality of its search engine.

"Privacy: 8 New Year's Resolutions for Protecting Your Privacy Online." ComputerUser.com Web site. Available online. URL: http://www.computeruser.com/articles/privacy-8-new-years-resolutions-for

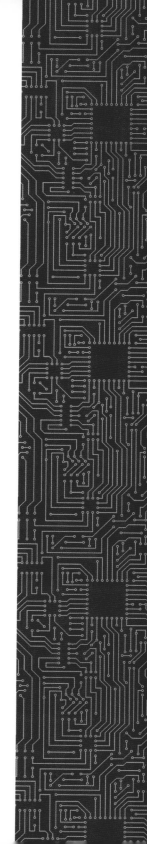

-protecting-your-privacy-online.html. Accessed July 5, 2011. Common-sense tips for securing your online accounts, including changing pass-words, unfriending people you do not know, and Googling yourself.

Schramm, Jennifer. "Privacy at Work." *HR Magazine.* Available online. URL: http://findarticles.com/p/articles/mi_m3495/is_4_50/ai_n13648822/ ?tag=content;col1. Accessed July 5, 2011. Do organizations have a right to monitor employee computer activity? Human Resources professionals say yes, employees say no.

Tynan, Daniel. "Your Boss Is Watching." PCWorld. Available online. URL: http://www.pcworld.com/article/118072/your_boss_is_watching.html. Accessed July 5, 2011. Experts debunk 10 myths about workplace privacy.

"Your Right to Privacy and Why You Won't Get It." Literary Nobody Web site. Available online. URL: http://www.literarynobody.com/2010/07/series -your-online-life-part-3-your-right-to-privacy-and-why-you-wont-get-it. html. Accessed July 5, 2011. Highlights the dangers of the lapse in privacy legislation.

WEB SITES

Avoidr. Available online. URL: http://www.avoidr.org/. Accessed July 5, 2011. This site warns you when certain Foursquare users are headed toward your venue, so you can duck out before they see you.

Demand Your dotRights. Available online. URL: http://www.dotrights.org. Accessed July 5, 2011. This ACLU site encourages users to demand the same privacy rights for the Internet that they have for telephone and other communication devices.

PleaseRobMe.com. Available online. URL: http://www.pleaserobme.com. Accessed July 5, 2011. Compares using geo-tracking services like Four-square to wearing a nametag that says "Please Steal This Smartphone."

"Computer Viruses: Invisible Threats to Privacy"

ARTICLES

King, Mark. "A Working Life: The Computer Virus Expert." *Guardian.* Available online. URL: http://www.guardian.co.uk/money/2010/aug/28/ computer-virus-expert-working-life. Accessed July 5, 2011. The biography of a Symantec security expert.

Krebs, Brian. "A Short History of Computer Viruses and Attacks." *Washington Post.* Available online. URL: http://www.washingtonpost.com/ac2/wp-dyn/A50636-2002Jun26. Accessed July 5, 2011. A chronology of the most devastating computer viruses in history.

"Man Charged with Unleashing 'Melissa' Computer Virus." CNN. Available online. URL: http://edition.cnn.com/TECH/computing/9904/02/melissa.arrest.03/index.html. Accessed July 5, 2011. The article describes the motive, means, and opportunity of the hacker who unleashed one of the most devastating worms in history.

Potter, Ned. "Top 10 Computer Viruses and Worms." ABC News. Available online. URL: http://abcnews.go.com/Technology/top-computer-viruses-worms-internet-history/story?id=8480794. Accessed July 5, 2011. Security experts at Symantec provide a list of the greatest viral threats to the Internet from the past four decades. The list reads: I Love You (2000), Conflicker (2009), Melissa (1999), Slammer (2003), Nimda (2001), Code Red (2001), Blaster (2003), Sasser (2004), Storm (2007), and Morris (1988).

Sutter, John D. "Experts: Malicious programs target Macs." CNN. Available online. URL: http://articles.cnn.com/2009-04-22/tech/first.mac.botnet_1_apple-computers-harmful-programs-botnet?_s=PM:TECH. Accessed July 5, 2011. Though Mac computers are nearly immune to computer viruses, a handful of harmful viruses released in 2009 targeted these machines.

"What Is a Computer Virus?" Microsoft Web site. Available online. URL: http://www.microsoft.com/security/pc-security/virus-whatis.aspx. Accessed July 5, 2011. This Microsoft article gives a brief description of computer viruses and how they are spread.

"Who Writes Computer Viruses?" Computer Sight Web site. Available online. URL: http://computersight.com/communication-networks/security/who-writes-computer-viruses/. Accessed July 5, 2011. The psychology of the digital vandals, professional programmers, and foreign intelligence operatives that produce computer viruses.

WEB SITES

Anatomy of a Virus. Available online. URL: http://chem.pitt.edu/facilities/virus_anatomy_poster.pdf. Accessed July 5, 2011. This poster shows how computer viruses are contracted, spread, and remedied.

"Spyware: Software Snooping on Your Private Data"

ARTICLES

Bradley, Tony. "Protect Yourself from Spyware." About.com Web site. Available online. URL: http://netsecurity.about.com/cs/generalsecurity/a/aa050204.htm. Accessed July 5, 2011. Simple tips everyone can use to protect themselves from spyware.

Coustan, Dave. "How Spyware Works." HowStuffWorks.com Web site. Available online. URL: http://computer.howstuffworks.com/spyware.htm. Accessed July 5, 2011. A description of common types of spyware, how it infects a computer, and what users can do to stop it.

Derene, Glenn. "Is Your Boss Spying on You? Inside New Workplace Surveillance." Popular Mechanics. Available online. URL: http://www.popularmechanics.com/technology/gadgets/news/4223564. Accessed July 5, 2011. Common techniques that employers use to (legally) spy on their employees.

Honeycutt, Jerry. "How to Protect Your Computer from Spyware and Adware." Microsoft.com Web site. Available online. URL: http://www.microsoft.com/windowsxp/using/security/expert/honeycutt_spyware.mspx. Accessed July 5, 2011. Tips from Microsoft on keeping your computer free of spyware and adware.

Landesman, Mary. "How to Remove Adware and Spyware." About.com Web site. Available online. URL: http://antivirus.about.com/od/spywareandadware/tp/adwarespyware.htm. Accessed July 5, 2011. Tips from About.com on removing spyware from an infected computer.

Nakamura, David. "9 D.C. Workers Fired For Looking at Porn." Washington Post. Available online. URL: http://www.washingtonpost.com/wp-dyn/content/article/2008/01/23/AR2008012302511.html?wpisrc=_rsstechnology. Accessed July 5, 2011. The story of employers who use company resources to snoop on the browsing habits of their employees while at work. This should be a cautionary tale for anyone who thinks it is okay to check Facebook while on the clock!

Olsen, Stefanie. "Clueless About Cookies or Spyware?" CNET News Web site. Available online. URL: http://news.cnet.com/Clueless-about-cookies-or-spyware/2100-1029_3-5561063.html. Accessed July 5, 2011. CNET explains the difference in cookies and spyware. Cookies help Internet sites track your activity, but any user can remove them or disable them at any time. Spyware often refuses to let its users remove it from the system.

Roberts, Paul. "Your PC May Be Less Secure Than You Think." PCWorld. Available online. URL: http://www.pcworld.com/article/118311/your_pc_may_be_less_secure_than_you_think.html. Accessed July 5, 2011. PCWorld discusses the startling statistics that over 20 percent of home computers are infected with a virus, worm, or spyware.

"What Is Spyware?" Microsoft.com Web site. Available online. URL: http://www.microsoft.com/security/spyware/whatis.aspx. Accessed July 5, 2011. Microsoft safety and security experts discuss spyware and how to avoid it.

WEB SITES

SpywareGuide. Available online. URL: http://www.spywareguide.com. Accessed July 5, 2011. This site provides a list of all known spyware and adware programs to be referenced when a program is suspected of sending information about usage back to its server.

"Phishing and Social Engineering: Confidence Games Go Online"

ARTICLES

Bright, Mat. "Online Identity Theft. Spoof Email Phishing Scams and Fake Web Pages or Sites." Miller Smiles Web site. Available online. URL: http://www.millersmiles.co.uk/identitytheft/gonephishing.htm. Accessed July 5, 2011. Discusses common phishing scams and social engineering tricks that users may fall victim to online.

Cranor, Lorrie Faith. "How to Foil 'Phishing' Scams." Scientific American. Available online. URL: http://www.scientificamerican.com/article.cfm?id=how-to-foil-phishing-scams. Accessed July 5, 2011. Understanding the human factors that can make secure networks vulnerable.

Jagatic, Tom et al. "Social Phishing." Indiana University. Available online. URL: http://www.indiana.edu/~phishing/social-network-experiment/phishing-preprint.pdf. Accessed July 5, 2011. Indiana University psychology professors conduct an experiment to determine how susceptible students are to phishing when the requests seem to come from a trusted source.

Legon, Jeordan. "'Phishing' scams reel in your identity." CNN. Available online. URL: http://articles.cnn.com/2003-07-21/tech/phishing.scam_1_ phishing-scam-artists-brand-spoofing?_s=PM:TECH. Accessed July 5, 2011. Shows how users are duped into providing personal information by techniques like brand spoofing, carding, and phishing.

McDonough, Molly. "Law Firms Swindled Out of $500K in E-Mail Scam." ABA Journal Web site. Available online. URL: http://www.abajournal. com/mobile/comments/honolulu_law_firms_swindled_out_of_500k_in_ e-mail_scam/. Accessed July 5, 2011. Honolulu law firms were the target of a Nigerian scam that cost over half a million dollars.

Mills, Elinor. "Social Engineering 101: Mitnick and Other Hackers Show How It's Done." CNet Web site. Available online. URL: http://news.cnet. com/8301-1009_3-9995253-83.html. Accessed July 5, 2011. During the Hackers on Planet Earth convention, Kevin Mitnick and a panel of other hackers discussed several of their social engineering ploys.

Moscaritolo, Angela. "Waledac Botnet Operators Amass 500,000 E-mail Credentials." *SC Magazine.* Available online. URL: http://www.scmagazineus. com/waledac-botnet-operators-amass-500000-email-credentials/article/ 195582/. Accessed July 5, 2011. The hackers operating the botnet "Waledac" have discovered over 500,000 e-mail addresses that will likely be used to deliver spam.

Mulrean, Jennifer. "Phishing Scams: How to Avoid Getting Hooked." MSN Money. Available online. URL: http://moneycentral.msn.com/content/ savinganddebt/consumeractionguide/p102559.asp. Accessed July 5, 2011. Tips to avoid being victimized by online phishing e-mails.

Posey, Brien. "How to Avoid Phishing Scams." WindowSecurity.com Web site. Available online. URL: http://www.windowsecurity.com/articles/Avoid -Phishing.html. Accessed July 5, 2011. The anatomy of a phishing attempt and why it often works.

Suciu, Peter. "The Basics: What Is Phishing?" Inc.com Web site. Available online. URL: http://technology.inc.com/security/articles/200609/ phishing.html. Accessed July 5, 2011. What can companies do to avoid becoming the victims of phishing attempts as employees unwittingly divulge private corporate information?

"Your Personal Information Online: Everyone Is a Public Figure Now"

ARTICLES

Heussner, Ki Mae. "10 of the Top Data Breaches of the Decade." ABC News Web site. Available online. URL: http://abcnews.go.com/Technology/Media/10-top-data-breaches-decade/story?id=10905634. Accessed July 5, 2011. A number of top security experts consider the devastating effects of some of the worst data breaches in the last decade.

"How to Remove Your Personal Information from Google and Internet." Available online. URL: http://www.squidoo.com/personalInformation. Accessed July 5, 2011. Several options for removing your information from search engines.

McCandlish, Stanton. "EFF's Top 12 Ways to Protect Your Online Privacy." Electronic Frontier Foundation Web site. Available online. URL: https://www.eff.org/wp/effs-top-12-ways-protect-your-online-privacy. Accessed July 5, 2011. The EFF technology director offers some commonsense advice to avoiding snoopers, including clearing cookies regularly and being aware of sites that might be harvesting your information.

WEB SITES

Spokeo.com. Available online. URL: http://www.spokeo.com. Accessed July 5, 2011. Spokeo collects and stores information from Facebook, Twitter, and other services to identify addresses, phone numbers, income, house values, and a plethora of other information, most willingly entered into social networking sites.

"Identity Theft: Protecting Oneself against Imposters"

ARTICLES

Feeley, Jef, and Van Voris, Bob. "Hacker Gets 20 Years in Largest Identity-Theft Case." Bloomberg (March 25, 2010). Available online. URL: http://www.bloomberg.com/apps/news?pid=newsarchive&sid=aCDo3co5A0Zk. Accessed July 5, 2011. Reports sentencing details of Albert Gonzalez's identity theft case.

Greenberg, Andy. "ID Theft: Don't Take It Personally." Forbes.com. Available online. URL: http://www.forbes.com/2010/02/09/banks-consumers -fraud-technology-security-id-theft.html. Accessed July 5, 2011. Reports on identity theft trends of the past decade.

Griffith, Eric. "Password Protection: Password Recovery and Control Tools." PCMag.com. Available online. URL: http://www.pcmag.com/ article2/0,2817,2368988,00.asp. Accessed July 5, 2011. Reviews common password management software.

"LexisNexis Theft Much Worse Than Thought." Associated Press. Available online. URL: http://www.msnbc.msn.com/id/7475594. Accessed July 5, 2011. Reports details of the March 2004 theft of the personal information of 310,000 people from the data broker.

Raphael, J. R. "Massive Identity Theft Exposes Troubling Trend." *PC World*. Available online. URL: http://www.pcworld.com/article/149485/massive_ identity_theft_exposes_troubling_trend. Accessed July 5, 2011. Reports on common identity theft issues.

Sullivan, Bob. "All Veterans at Risk of ID Theft After Data Heist." NBC News. Available online. URL: www.msnbc.msn.com/id/12916803/ns/technology_ and_science-security/. Accessed July 5, 2011. Reports on theft of personal information from Veterans Administration.

WEB SITES

Federal Trade Commission. Available online. URL: www.ftc.gov. Accessed July 5, 2011. Federal government's consumer protection site.

TrustE.com. Available online. URL: http://www.truste.com. Accessed July 5, 2011. Web site for the online privacy certification company.

United States Department of Justice. Available online. URL: www.justice. gov. Accessed July 5, 2011. Web site for the federal department responsible for the enforcement of the law.

"Keeping Your Data Secure: The Best Offense Is a Good Defense"

ARTICLES

Blight, Garry, and Sheila Pulham. "Arab spring: an interactive timeline of Middle East protests." Available online. URL: http://www.guardian.co.uk/ world/interactive/2011/mar/22/middle-east-protest-interactive-timeline.

Accessed September 30, 2011. An interactive time line of protests, government actions, and international responses to the various political actions in 2011 now known as the "Arab Spring." Clyman, John. "Secure Your Data," PCMag.com. Available online. URL: http://www.consumersearch.com/online-backup-services/important-features. Accessed July 5, 2011. A guide to software and tools that protect systems and data.

Cox, John. "Mobile Users Face Knotty Security Issues." Network World. Available online. URL: http://www.networkworld.com/news/2006/071706-mobile-users-security.html?page=3. Accessed July 5, 2011. High-profile security breaches in the brave new world of mobile computing.

Fitzpatrick, Jason. "Five Best File Encryption Tools." Lifehacker. Available online. URL: http://lifehacker.com/5677725/five-best-file-encryption-tools. Accessed July 5, 2011. Readers rank their favorite encryption tools.

Geier, Eric. "Mobile Security Tips for Encrypting USB Flash Drives," Enterprise Mobile Today.com, May 28, 2010. Available online. URL: http://www.enterprisemobiletoday.com//article.php/3884916. Accessed July 5, 2011. Simple steps for protecting data on a flash drive.

Ide, William. "Analysts: Stuxnet Raises Concerns About Vulnerability of Nuclear, Industrial Facilities." Voice of America.com, September 28, 2010. Available online. URL: http://www.voanews.com/english/news/middle-east/Analysts-Stuxnet-Raises-Concerns-About-Vulnerability-of-Nuclear-Industrial-Facilties-103963943.html. Accessed July 5, 2011. Reports on a powerful computer virus that apparently infected computer systems worldwide.

Kant, Chander, and Dmitri Joukovski. "Top Considerations for Implementing Secure Backup and Recovery." Zmanda Open Source Backup. Available online. URL: http://www.zmanda.com/backup-security.html. Accessed July 5, 2011. Reports on how corporate security policies often neglect backup procedures.

Mehling, Herman. "Top Six Mobile Security Threats and How to Prevent Them." Enterprise Mobile Today.com, August 27, 2010. Available online. URL: http://www.enterprisemobiletoday.com/features/security/article.php/3900806/Top-Six-Mobile-Security-Threats-and-How-to-Prevent-Them.htm. Accessed July 5, 2011/. As smartphone use increases, security threats are multiplying.

Meredith, Leslie. "How to Protect Your Laptop in Public Places." Tech News Daily, November 1, 2010. Available online. URL: http://www.technews daily.com/how-to-protect-your-laptop-in-public-places-1542. Accessed July 5, 2011. Laptops' portability comes with vulnerabilities.

Ryan, Patrick S. "War, Peace, or Stalemate: Wargames, Wardialing, Wardriving, and the Emerging Market for Hacker Ethics." *Virginia Journal of Law & Technology* 9, no. 7 (Summer 2004). Available online. URL: http://ssrn. com/abstract=585867. Accessed July 5, 2011. Examines the argument that the act of wardriving can be beneficial to society.

Tweney, Dylan. "The Hidden Downside of Wireless Networking." District Administration, June 2006. Available online. URL: http://www.district administration.com/viewarticle.aspx?rticleid=207&p=2#0. Accessed July 5, 2011. Tips for keeping a wireless network safe.

WEB SITES

Microsoft Online Safety. Available online. URL: http://www.microsoft.com/ protect/default.aspx. Accessed July 5, 2011. Online safety and privacy information from the software giant.

Online Tech Tips.com. Available online. URL: http://www.online-tech-tips. com/free-software-downloads/encrypt-and-password-protect-text-files -for-free/. Accessed July 5, 2011. A blog that provides computer tips.

Wi-Fi Alliance.org. Available online. URL: http://www.wi-fi.org/. Accessed July 5, 2011. Site of the trade association that owns the Wi-Fi trademark and promotes wireless technology and security.

Wisegeek.com. Available online. URL: http://www.wisegeek.com/what-is -encryption.htm. Accessed July 5, 2011. Web site that answers reader-submitted questions.

"Databases, Privacy, and Security: Monitoring the Online You"

BOOKS

Alderman, Ellen, and Caroline Kennedy. *The Right to Privacy.* New York: Vintage Books, 1997. Alderman and Kennedy present the legal conflicts that resulted in our shrinking right to privacy.

ARTICLES

Anderson, Nate. "Anonymized Data Really Isn't—and Here's Why Not." Ars Technica. Available online. URL: http://arstechnica.com/tech-policy/news/2009/09/your-secrets-live-online-in-databases-of-ruin.ars. Accessed July 5, 2011. A computer expert shows that 87 percent of Americans can be identified by their zip code, birthdate, and sex.

Bell, Gordon, and Jim Gemmell. "A Digital Life." *Scientific American.* Available online. URL: http://www.scientificamerican.com/article.cfm?id=a-digital-life. Accessed July 5, 2011. New systems may allow people to record everything they see and hear.

Cherry, Steven. "Total Recall." *IEEE Spectrum* magazine. Available online. URL: http://spectrum.ieee.org/telecom/security/total-recall. Accessed July 5, 2011. Gordon Bell attempts to record everything about his life in his MyLifeBits project.

"DNA Database Will Span Most of the UK Population." Available online. URL: http://www.theregister.co.uk/2007/04/11/dna_database/. Accessed July 5, 2011. Discusses the genetics databases available in England.

"Genetic Discrimination: A Position Paper Presented by the Council for Responsible Genetics." Available online. URL: http://www.councilforresponsiblegenetics.org/ViewPage.aspx?pageId=85. Accessed July 5, 2011. Genetic tests can be used to help and harm. This article discusses some of the negative effects of genetic testing.

Lucky, Robert. "Life Bits." IEEE Spectrum Magazine. Available online. URL: http://www.boblucky.com/reflect/may05.htm. Accessed July 5, 2011. Commentary on Gordon Bell's "Life Bits" project.

McCullagh, Declan. "Database Nation: The Upside of Zero Privacy." Reason.com. Available online. URL: http://reason.com/archives/2004/06/01/database-nation. Accessed July 5, 2011. This editorial suggests that the benefits provided by unlimited database access to our lives far outweigh the risks associated with the loss of privacy.

United States Department of Commerce. "Commercial Data Privacy and Innovation in the Internet Economy: A Dynamic Policy Framework." Available online. URL: http://www.ntia.doc.gov/reports/2010/IPTF_Privacy_Green_Paper_12162010.pdf. Accessed July 5, 2011. This Department of Commerce report attempts to develop a sound Internet policy for the sharing of corporate data.

Wilkinson, Alec. "Remember This? A Project to Record Everything We Do in Life." *New Yorker.* Available online. URL: http://www.newyorker.com/reporting/2007/05/28/070528fa_fact_wilkinson#ixzz1C4mfO0iF. Accessed July 5, 2011. This *New Yorker* article discusses Gordon Bell's attempts at recording everything that happens to him.

WEB SITES

EPIC Web site. URL: http://epic.org/. Accessed July 5, 2011. The Electronic Privacy Information Center.

Federal Trade Commission. URL: http://www.ftc.gov/bcp/edu/microsites/idtheft/consumers/compromised.html. Accessed July 5, 2011. How to tell if you have been a victim of identity theft and the steps you should take.

Gordon Bell's Home Page. URL: http://research.microsoft.com/en-us/um/people/gbell/. Accessed July 5, 2011. Gordon Bell's official home page.

JustAskGemalto.com. URL: https://www.justaskgemalto.com/. Accessed July 5, 2011. Cyber-security and data privacy activist.

Microsoft Research: URL: http://research.microsoft.com/en-us/projects/mylifebits/default.aspx. Accessed July 5, 2011. The MyLifeBits official site.

Reputation.com. URL: http://www.reputation.com/. Accessed July 5, 2011. Manages an online reputation by pushing positive reviews of a product to the tops of search engines.

INDEX

Italic page numbers indicate illustrations.